SAVED TO SERVE

Finding Your Purpose

Dr. Michael Landsman

COPYRIGHTS

ABOUT THE AUTHOR

Dr. Michael Landsman has been in full time ministry for 42 years and has served in various capacities during that time span, functioning as a Pastor; International Missions Director; Missionary; Traveling Teaching Ministry; Licensed Pastoral Counselor; Educator; Bible College Dean; Chaplain for the Los Angeles Police Department; Ministry Consultant; and Author.

Further, Dr. Landsman was one of the original members of the International Churches and Ministers, as well as a founding trustee for Covenant Ministries International; and a Board Member of Fresh Oil Fellowship.

Dr. Landsman had been part of the Oral Roberts Educational Fellowship for the Bible School Division at its inception and taught a segment on Bible School Curriculum at their first Symposium.

Author of the National/World Outreach Bible School Curriculum, Dr. Landsman has overseen the establishment of schools in various countries with supporting material translated into French, Spanish, Portuguese, Norwegian, Polish, and Russian.

In addition, Dr. Landsman has authored several books that have also been translated into various languages. The titles are:

- **Supportive Ministries (The Supernatural Development of the Ministry of Helps);**
- **Attitude of a Servant**
- **Lord, Increase our Faith**
- **Doubling Your Ability through God**
- **Mercy, the Gift Before and Beyond Faith"** **(co-authored with Buddy Harrison)**

Dr. Landsman spent 11 years in South Africa teaching in Rhema Bible College. The last two years of his tenure, he was the Dean and Academic Head of the college. He is also the South African Director of Daystar Christian Television.

Founder and President of Michael Landsman Ministry Consulting, Dr. Landsman is working with Faith Fellowship, New Jersey, as the International Director for their Bible Schools (Faith International Training Schools)

He has been married to Martha for the past 42 years. They have three children and three grandchildren. Two of their children are in full time ministries of their own.

TABLE OF CONTENTS

COPYRIGHTS..ii

ABOUT THE AUTHOR...iii

TABLE OF CONTENTS..v

INTRODUCTION...vi

DEDICATION ix

SECTION 1 – *SUPPORTIVE MINISTRIES* x

CHAPTER 1   A Gift of God 1

CHAPTER 2   The Dream 6

CHAPTER 3   The Disciples...11

CHAPTER 4   The Early Church...18

CHAPTER 5   Be Faithful 24

CHAPTER 6   Rewards Of Faithfulness...................................31

CHAPTER 7   Keeping Clear of Strife 40

SECTION 2 – *ATTITUDE OF A SERVANT* 46

CHAPTER 1   The Right Attitude 47

CHAPTER 2   Saved to Serve...55

CHAPTER 3   The Mind of Christ 69

CHAPTER 4   The Parable of the Talents................................73

CHAPTER 5   Singleness of Heart..91

CHAPTER 6   Function of a Servant 99

CHAPTER 7   The Paradox of Greatness................................119

CHAPTER 8   The Example of Jesus.......................................128

CONCLUSION..136

A SPECIAL THANK YOU 138

BIBLIOGRAPHY 140

WORLD OUTREACH BIBLE SCHOOLS   (W. O. B. S.)................141

INTRODUCTION

FIRST THOUGHTS

In two distinct supernatural occurrences; a dream, and a divine visitation; the Lord revealed the truths that I am sharing with you in this book. If you grasp these truths, they will greatly impact, and revolutionize, your life, and productivity for the Kingdom of God.

In the Gospels, Jesus provides vivid examples of how we should live. In His teachings, He stressed the attitude of the heart. God looks on the intent of the heart more than the outcome of the actions.

" ... *For the Lord sees not as man sees; for man looks on the outward appearance, but the Lord looks on the heart.*" (*I Samuel 16:7(b)*)

Jesus shows us a true servant, one who was determined to do the will of God from the heart. He demonstrates that having a servant's heart is not a sign of weakness, but rather a sign of strength and inner peace.

I am the type of individual who loves a challenge, even when it requires change on my part. I have found that God expects us to grow and that means change. While change is mandatory, we must keep in mind that the principles of God remain constant. The methods of enacting those principles are variable and change with the dynamics of society, but the principles remain constant.

Sociology tells us that our society is reinventing itself every 3-5 years. Have we in the Church kept pace with these changes? New methods do not necessarily change principles, but rather give us an opportunity to impact, win, and train people in a relevant way.

Television is a classic example of this principle. Seventy years ago the idea of spreading the Gospel by television was absurd, but today television is a very practical and efficient tool for evangelism. The change was not in God or in His principles, but rather in our modern technology. Television, which at one time was considered a "tool of the devil," is now reaching millions of people with the Gospel. It has enabled us to be more effective in carrying out the Great Commission--to preach the Gospel to the entire world.

It is challenging to look at your lifestyle and service for the King, and determine if your attitude and actions are equal to each other. One's actions must always be in correspondence to the proper attitude.

You can never be a true servant until you know your rights and privileges as well as your responsibilities. In Christian terms, a good servant completely identifies with the Master. To properly represent his master, a servant must be familiar with all that his master is. The servant's attitude directly affects his ability to serve his master in any situation.

Likewise, your attitude is one of the most vital aspects of your Christian life. Your attitude must be right in everything you do so that the Master's perfect will can be carried out.

It is my intent through this book, to help you grow into all God has for you to be and do. That means continual upward movement, along with the proper attitude. I am confident that, as you read this book, you will be enlightened by the Holy Spirit on how to be more productive in the Kingdom of God, while maintaining the *Attitude of a Servant*.

DEDICATION

In the process of writing a book, it is important to have those surrounding you who believe in you and what you are writing. They keep you encouraged and covered with prayer.

In my life that person is my wife, Martha. She always has been my greatest fan and encourager. She is the one who is called along side of me. She is the one who continues to say; "keep at it; you can do it." She, above all others, is a great example of living the lifestyle of, and having the *Attitude of a Servant*.

SECTION 1 – *SUPPORTIVE MINISTRIES*

CHAPTER 1   A Gift of God

I want to share with you some precepts from the Word of God that have greatly ministered to me. These precepts concern what I call Supportive Ministries. They have helped me, over the years, to understand the important and vital role every member of the Body of Christ plays in the success of any ministry or church.

SUPPORTIVE MINISTRIES

If you have ever been involved in a supportive type of ministry, you have probably had the opportunity to fight off the temptation to quit or complain. I believe that if you will allow God's Word to minister to your heart in this area, you will find peace and be liberated.

"And God hath set some in the church, first apostles, secondarily prophets, thirdly teachers, after that miracles, then gifts of healings, helps, governments, diversities of tongues.

Are all apostles? Are all prophets? Are all teachers? Are all workers of miracles? Do all interpret?

But covet earnestly the best gifts: and yet show I unto you a more excellent way." (I Corinthians 12: 28-31)

"And he gave some apostles; and some prophets; and some, evangelists; and some, pastors and teachers; for the perfecting of the saints, for the work of the ministry, for the edifying of the body of Christ." (Ephesians 4: 11, 12)

God has set gifts in the Church: apostles, prophets, evangelists, pastors and teachers for the perfecting (maturing) of the saints, for the work of the ministry [the saints are to do the work of service], for the edifying of the body of Christ. But in addition to these five-fold ministry gifts, there are also helps, governments, and diversities of tongues.

In these Scriptures, we see that the ministry of helps is not necessarily part of what has been classified as the five-fold ministry. These are separate but vital ministries. The same is true for the ministry of governments. However, in certain situations, these individual gifts may operate together. For instance, in the pastor's ministry, governments will enter in because a pastor must be able to govern his church.

God has set certain ministries in the Church to fulfill **one primary function: to serve in a supportive role.** *Helps* and *governments* were instituted by God to do just that. They are supportive ministries.

Each of us is called to be a witness for Jesus, to share the Gospel with our neighbors; however not all are called into a five-fold gift ministry such as an apostle, prophet, evangelist, pastor, or teacher. Some, who are called to these positions, are still developing into that calling. This book is designed to encourage you to minister unto the Lord from the position you are in right now.

The word *support* can be defined as 'to uphold by aid; to assist as a subordinate character, (one who functions underneath to uphold another); to be able to supply the funds necessary to continue on.' It also means 'to assist or to further a cause; or to act as an aid or an attendant of someone or something.'

We can see this in every movie or television program. There is a star – a leading man or leading lady; but there are also supporting characters. Each year, Academy Awards are presented for Best Actor and Best Actress, and also for Best Supporting Actor and Actress.

The function of these supporting actors and actresses is vital to the success of the show and are designed to make the star of the show look good and perform at their maximum efficiency. The star would be unable to accomplish his or her task if it were not for all those involved in a supportive capacity in the show. This is true even for the person who walks on camera to say only one word.

Everyone has a part to play. Without all these supporting characters, the show could not progress. One person can't do it all!

The same is true with the Gospel. God did not call one person and say, 'Okay, this is what I want you to do, and you get to do it all by yourself.' No, God has set in the Church certain ministries and ministry gifts to perform specific jobs and to carry out specific tasks. Just as a pastor is pastor, not only to the local church, but to the Body of Christ in general, so also do those in supportive roles minister to the entire Body. And all of us are ministering unto the Lord.

When a person is initially called into the ministry, they immediately want to rush out and function in that ministry. Very often, they move out ahead of God because they fail to realize that it will take a time of preparation, before the Word has renewed their minds and saturated their spirits. Failure and discouragement is the result, and many times they just give up and want to quit.

This was a mistake I made early in my ministry. I was tired of being an assistant. I had made up my mind that since God had called me to preach, I was going to preach! So I jumped out ahead of God and, because I was unprepared, I experienced some setbacks. I was fortunate enough to have a wise pastor who was there to encourage me to continue to press forward. I had to find out where I missed it. I had to go back and complete the job God had for me before I could move out into the ministry God called me to.

When the Lord had directed me to move to Tulsa, Oklahoma, I had a few questions. I approached the Lord without any preconceived religious ideas. In fact it was tongue in cheek. I said: "I know why you want me to go to Tulsa, to teach faith and healing because Kenneth Hagin, Oral Roberts, and T L Osborne were not enough." (Yeah! Right!).

I wanted God to tell me that it was because of a strong anointing or a great teaching ability that he was sending me to Tulsa. Instead the Lord spoke to my heart and said to me: "I am sending you there, not because of your anointing or teaching ability, but because I know that you will not only start a process, but you will stay with it until it is completed." In other words, he was sending me there because I would not quit or give up. I would remain until the assignment was completed.

Since that time, I have learned quite a bit about supportive ministries, your attitude, and the vital part they play in the Body of Christ. In the ensuing chapters, I will attempt to impart what I have learned to you, that the eyes of your understanding might be enlightened; that you will know the hope to which you have been called, and be comfortable fitting into that place of service.

CHAPTER 2   The Dream

TRUE TO THE VISION

Have you ever been discouraged and wondering if all you had heard and been taught was really worth it? You see the seeming rapid success of others, but do not see it for yourself? If so, you can identify with where I was at in the early part of my ministry. I had come to a point of frustration and almost hopelessness. I had seen many problems and pitfalls that had hindered other ministries. I did not want to follow in the same vein, but I began to think that there was no future for me, except serving in the capacity I was in. So I questioned the Lord concerning what direction He had for my life and ministry.

One night, I had a dream – a spiritual dream- totally in line with God's Word (*Acts 2:17*). In this dream, the Lord showed me a man who had been given a job to do. As he proceeded to carry out that vision, the Lord added other people, with the skills needed, to help him get the job done.

I asked the Lord, "Why do some people have visions of large ministries and others do not?" In answer, He began to speak to me about supportive ministries. Each of us has a specific task God has laid on our hearts, but some of these jobs require the aid and support of others.

The church I served in California is an example of this. The senior pastor and visionary was called by God to do a specific job. In a vision, he saw a large building where thousands of people were seated, receiving the Word of God. He saw other buildings, one of which was a Bible training Center. The Lord showed him various other phases of ministry such as radio and television outreaches, evangelistic crusades, and a monthly magazine.

The senior pastor knew that to accomplish what was shown him was physically impossible for one man to carry. Did God make a mistake in showing him all that He wanted him to do? No. God brought in the supportive ministers – men and women - who had the skills and abilities to accomplish all the tasks that would be required to be used in specific areas to get the job done.

In the natural realm, there is no way one man could do all the work involved in running a multi-faceted ministry. It requires the aid and support of other men and women of God; people who are called and anointed of God to fill a supportive role.

Just imagine how it would be if one man had to do every job all by himself: handle the radio and television outreaches, run the Christian school; set up the evangelistic crusades; and supervise the Bible training center. Then every Sunday, he would have to make sure the Sunday school department was operating properly, teach all classes; lead the worship service; sing a special song; preach, pray, prophesy, minister to the sick; close the service; and then clean up afterward!

One man cannot do all those jobs alone. God sent various individuals to the church to help accomplish the tasks. He provided assistant and associate pastors for the church, an administrator for the Bible training center; an associate evangelist for the crusade outreach, and many others.

Many people get excited when they hear of such a vision. They want to get involved but, too many times, they only want to be in the "spotlight." They believe they are to minister alongside the man of God, teaching with him and praying for the sick. They expect to start at the top and are unwilling to do anything less. If they would catch the vision, they would see their part in it. Jesus said those who are faithful in the little things shall be made rulers over much (*Matthew 25:21; Luke 19:17*).

AS YOU THINK YOU BECOME

People who work in a ministry should look upon their jobs as more than a means of financial supply. They are dedicated to that ministry. It is their calling. Secretaries are not just secretaries, they are called of God to work there. They freely stay after hours on their own time, getting their job done and doing it right for God. They may be called to fill the office of teacher or evangelist in the future, but meanwhile, they are serving the Lord and getting the Word out. They are supporting the leader God has placed helping him fulfill his calling.

In fact even the church receptionist is a vital part in the fulfilling of the vision. They are not 'just a receptionist' but rather the central nervous system of the ministry. They have been entrusted with the responsibility of making sure that those who call or come in are directed to the proper person to have their needs met. The receptionist is vital to that person getting the help they need. It is an awesome responsibility and they should see themselves in that manner.

In Proverbs 23:7(a) states, *"For as a man thinks in his heart, so is he..."* In other words, the way you see yourself is what you will become. You will rise to the level of expectation you have for yourself, or that others have of you.

Every person is vital to the proper functioning of a ministry. All of them must be in agreement and speak the same thing. The Apostle Paul wrote, *"Now I beseech you, brethren, by the name of the Lord Jesus Christ, that you all speak the same thing, and that there be no divisions among you; but that you be perfectly joined together in the same mind and in the same judgment."* (*I Corinthians 1:10*).

They must operate in love and always believe the best about one another. When each part functions properly, the whole ministry operates smoothly (see *I Corinthians 12: 14-26*). As I began to realize the importance of these supportive ministries, the Lord showed me how this worked in His own ministry.

CHAPTER 3   The Disciples

"And when he had called unto him his twelve disciples, he gave them power against unclean spirits, to cast them out, and to heal all manner of sickness and disease...

These twelve Jesus sent forth, and commanded them, saying...As ye go, preach, saying, the kingdom of heaven is at hand. Heal the sick, cleanse the lepers, raise the dead, cast out devils; freely ye have received, freely give.

He that receives you receives me...He that receives a prophet in the name of a prophet shall receive a prophet's reward; and he that receives a righteous man in the name of a righteous man shall receive a righteous man's reward".

(Matthew 10: 1-8, 40, 41)

In these Scriptures, Jesus sent forth His disciples to cast out demons, heal all manner of sickness and disease, preach, cleanse the lepers, and raise the dead.

This is an exciting part of ministry, to watch God perform signs and wonders as you minister His Word. This is a part of the ministry everyone seems to want, but few seem to have read what took place before Jesus' disciples went forth to do these things.

These twelve were called to be apostles, but they did not start out that way. Jesus called them and set them apart with one specific purpose in mind. That purpose was to carry out the work of the Gospel after He left and sent the Holy Spirit. He called them and gave them power to cast out devils, to heal all manner of sickness and disease, to cleanse the lepers, to raise the dead, and to preach that the Kingdom of God was at hand.

They were called to that level of ministry, but before Jesus gave them this power, the majority of their time was taken up with what many today would consider menial work. They were sent out in the power of God and did exploits in His Name, only to return, and continue doing menial work. I cannot find one recorded instance where any of them complained about what they were doing. They were excited to be a part of what God was doing, to be involved in the move of God.

Throughout the Gospels, the twelve disciples were with the Lord constantly. They traveled with Him everywhere. They made preparations before Jesus ministered, probably controlled the healing lines, and cleaned up after the meetings were over.

MIRACLES REQUIRE ALL FUNCTIONING

In *Matthew 14: 16-20*, we find an account of Jesus feeding five thousand men (plus woman and children), Notice that He told the disciples, *"Give ye them to eat."* According to Mark's Gospel, the disciples had the people sit in groups or ranks, by hundreds and by fifties (*Mark 6:40*).

Jesus blessed the loaves and fishes; then gave them to the disciples. It was the disciples who distributed the food to the multitude. It was the disciples who did the clean-up work ... *and they (the disciples) took up the fragments that remained, twelve baskets full. (Matthew 14:20)*

We have read this passage of Scripture and been excited about Jesus feeding over five thousand people with only five loaves and two fishes, but there is one thing we have missed. These are the **same disciples** who previously had been used by God to perform **miracles**. After this, they went back to performing what could bee seen as menial tasks. In one moment they were used in the working of a miracle and in the next moment back to the normal and mundane work.

When Jesus commanded the people to be seated in ranks of hundreds and fifties, who supervised the seating? The disciples did. When Jesus blessed the bread and broke it, who gave it to the people? The disciples were the ones who passed out the food to the people. Not only did the disciples wait on the people making sure everyone was fed, but when it was done, they had to do the clean-up work.

Jesus had just performed a great miracle. The people were excited. But here were the disciples, feeding everyone and then cleaning up the mess that was left! When they had finished the clean-up chores, did Jesus say to them, "Oh that was a good job men; take a rest. Take three days off if you need them?" No! He told them to get into the boat and row to the other side of the sea. *(Mathew14:22)*.

Here is something for you to consider from *Mark 6:39-42*. It took everyone doing their job to accomplish the miracle. First the disciples *(the 12, Matthew 10:2-4; and the 72 others, Luke 10:1)*, had to sit the people in groups of 50's and 100's. Then Jesus blessed and broke the loaves and fishes into enough for the 12 who in turn divided it to the 72 others, who in turn divided it to the people. They all then had to clean up afterwards and give an accounting of what was left over. Each one had a specific part to play in the accomplishing of the miracle. The bread and fish multiplied through all their hands, working together to meet the needs of the people.

These men had been working three days and three nights—taking care of the people, handling the prayer lines, feeding the multitudes, cleaning up the mess. Then, they had to row across the sea!

We find a similar situation in Mark's Gospel:

And when they had sent away the multitude, they took him even as he was in the ship. And there were also with him other little ships. And there arose a great storm of wind, and the waves beat into the ship, so that it was now full. And he was in the hinder part of the ship asleep on a pillow. (Mark 4:36-38)

Can you imagine that? The disciples had been working throughout the crusade, working to the point of fatigue – and what does Jesus do? He goes to sleep in the back of the ship!

Here, we have a good opportunity for a case of self-pity. The disciples could have said, "Oh, poor us! We have worked so hard during the crusade – organizing, ushering, and keeping everything decent and in order. Now we have to row to the other side of the sea. Look at Him! He doesn't even care. He's sleeping in the back of the boat. We did all the work. All He did was preach, pray for the sick, and work miracles. We did all the work and He gets all the glory! Oh, poor us!"

By the time they had rowed to the middle of the sea, a storm was raging and they had the chance to cry and complain all the more! Finally, they woke Jesus and said, *"Master, carest thou not that we perish?" (Mark 4:38).*

Jesus stood, rebuked the wind, and said: *"Peace; be still!"* Then He turned and rebuked the disciples. He said, *"Why are ye so fearful? How is it that ye have no faith?" (Mark 4:40).*

In *Matthew 21:1-7*, Jesus sent the disciples to get a donkey for His triumphant entry into

Jerusalem. He didn't say, "Men, you've been working so hard with me. Let's get a whole fleet of donkeys and ride into Jerusalem together." No! He said, "Get one for me," and they did as He commanded.

What did they do then? They put their clothes on the colt for Jesus to sit on. They didn't cry and complain. They didn't ask, "When are we going to be exalted?" No one asked, "When am I going to get called up front to preach?" They were excited about what God was doing and excited to be a part of it.

The disciples operated in a supportive role, in a supportive ministry. They had gone out and ministered the Word. They had seen signs and wonders take place in their ministries, and they were excited about it. But, when they returned, they continued to do what God had called them to do. Their support, their aid, and assistance helped the Lord's ministry flow smoothly. They supported the ministry God had placed them in. They got involved and were excited about doing God's work. Even though the majority of their work was what most people would consider menial, they were faithful to do it and everything ran like clockwork.

If you are involved in a ministry, you need to grasp the importance of your job. **You are a vital part of the ministry you support**, whether it is by actual physical work or with your prayers and finances. **It takes all working together to get the job done.** No one person is more important than another. All of us have a job to fulfill; it is our calling from God.

CHAPTER 4   The Early Church

Jesus chose twelve men to follow Him and work with Him in His ministry. Then in *Luke 10:1*, He appointed seventy-two others. After Judas Iscariot betrayed Jesus, he had to be replaced. This is recorded in *Acts 1: 15-26:*

And in those days Peter stood up in the midst of the disciples, and said, Men and brethren ... of these men which have companied with us all the time that the Lord Jesus went in and out among us, beginning from the baptism of John, unto that same day that he was taken up from us, must one be ordained to be a witness with us of his resurrection.

And they appointed two; Joseph called Barsabas, who was surnamed Justus, and Mathias. And they prayed, and said, Thou, Lord, which knowest the hearts of all, shew whether of these two thou hast chosen, that he may take part of this ministry and apostleship, from which Judas by transgression fell, that he might go to his own place.

And they gave forth their lots; and the lot fell upon Matthias; and he was numbered with the eleven apostles. (Acts 1: 15-26)

When Judas had to be replaced, what did the apostles do? They said, "Let's look among ourselves." They looked among the seventy that were with them from the very beginning and chose one from among that group.

Matthias was one of the disciples that had been with the Lord since His baptism in the Jordan River. He was not on the ministerial staff or on the teaching staff; he was just a member of the congregation. But I want you to understand one thing, God knew his heart. I believe Matthias got involved in anything there was to do and was excited about it because he was serving God. God knew his heart and exalted him from the position of disciple to that of apostle.

Matthias was not looking to be exalted. He was not fasting and praying, "Lord, make me an apostle like the others." If he had, God would never have exalted him. But because he was involved in what God was doing, God chose him and exalted him.

Remember: Get involved and do what there is to do. *God will exalt you*!

EXAMPLES

An excellent example of a supportive ministry is the deacon.

And in those days when the number of disciples was multiplied, there arose a murmuring of the Grecians against the Hebrews, because their widows were neglected in the daily ministration. Then the twelve called the multitude of the disciples unto them, and said, It is not right that we should leave the word of God, and serve tables.

Wherefore, brethren, look ye out among you seven men of honest report, full of the Holy Ghost and wisdom, who we may appoint over this business. But we will give ourselves continually to prayer, and to the ministry of the word.

And the saying pleased the whole multitude. And they chose (them)...and when they had prayed, they laid their hands on them. (Acts 6: 1-6)

Note again the qualifications of the deacon: (1) Full of the Holy Ghost; (2) Full of wisdom; and (3) Having an honest report among the people. The apostles set down the criteria for becoming a deacon, and the multitude chose the seven men they felt were most qualified. Then the apostles prayed and laid their hands on them, ordaining them into this ministry. They were being empowered for this service.

And the word of God increased; and the number of the disciples multiplied in Jerusalem greatly. (Acts 6:7)

Why was this possible? It became possible because men came in and took supportive positions. They took over the physical serving of tables and relieved the apostles to give themselves to the Word and to prayer. Because of this, the Word of God increased. The purity, clarity, and revelation of God's Word increased because the apostles were able to spend time in the Word, in prayer, in meditation, and praying in the Spirit. And the Church grew!

I am convinced that it is the same in any congregation today. We need to follow this Scriptural pattern. *As ministers are relieved of the physical care of their churches, as they give themselves to the Word and to prayer, the Word of God will increase.* The revelation knowledge will go forth and increase; and the church will grow.

As long as ministers always have to be involved in the menial work that needs to be done, the Word will never increase and their church will never grow.

If you are involved in a church or ministry and desire to see it grow, relieve the pastor (or person in charge) of the little things. Free him to spend time in prayer and in the Word. Not only will the church or ministry grown, but God will promote you as He promotes that ministry.

The deacons were called and anointed by God for that ministry, and they fulfilled it gladly. Philip may have had it in his heart to go out and preach the Gospel, but he started as a deacon (the ministry of helps). He began there, and God exalted him to the ministry of an evangelist.

The Word is full of examples of supportive ministries. In Acts 13, we read about Barnabas and Paul. They were teachers and prophets set in the church at Antioch, and they ministered there until the Lord promoted them to the ministry of apostles. You will notice in the Word that God exalted Barnabas and Paul into the ministry of apostles; they were no longer simply teachers and prophets.

When they left the church at Antioch, they were "Barnabas and Paul." When they returned, they were "Paul and Barnabas." In *Acts 14*, we see that Paul had become the chief speaker. It didn't bother Barnabas that Paul had been exalted and used by God in a mighty way. Barnabas had seen his potential and *helped* Paul develop his ministry.

Paul and Barnabas worked together, and God gave the increase. There was no strife or division between them. They complemented each other and the results were tremendous: A great multitude came to the Lord.

Throughout the Word, we find other supportive ministers: Silas, Titus, Aquila and Priscilla, Philemon, Timothy, and other men and women of God who helped support the Word with their time and their substance.

Luke, the physician, is an excellent example. His primary function was to travel with Paul and do everything necessary to make Paul comfortable. He was a supportive minister to Paul. In addition, he studied and interviewed people as a basis for what we know today as "The Gospel According to St. Luke." He recorded the history of the Church. I am sure he had opportunities to minister and pray for the sick, but that was not his primary function. He operated in the ministry God had called him to: a supportive ministry.

Timothy is another example. He traveled with Paul and was faithful. When Paul went on to Macedonia, he made Timothy overseer of the Church in Ephesus. In *Philippians 2: 19-23,* we read how much importance Paul placed upon Timothy:

"But I trust in the Lord Jesus to send Timothy shortly unto you, that I also may be of good comfort, when I know your state. For I have no man likeminded, who will naturally care for your state.

For all seek their own, not the things which are Jesus Christ's. But you know the proof of him, that, as a son with the father, he hath served with me in the gospel. Him therefore I hope to send presently, as soon as I shall see how it goes with me."

(Philippians 2: 19-23)

If you are called to minister the Gospel, I recommend that you get involved with a ministry that is putting out the Word of God to the world. Get involved with that ministry and help it any way you can. Be unselfish about it, and God will promote you right on time! (*See Proverbs 4:8; I Peter 5:6.*)

CHAPTER 5   Be Faithful

PREPARATION

It is important to realize that preparation is not lost time. Do not be overanxious and jump out ahead of God. It is a good idea to get involved in another's ministry and be faithful in what you do. Help another minister get their job done. Promote God's Word and God will promote you (*Proverbs 4:5-9*). You do not have to promote yourself; God will do that as you are faithful to what He has told you to do. *"Exalt her; and she shall promote you: she will bring you honor, when you embrace her." (Verse 8)*

As you read and meditate on the Word, the Lord will reveal this to you. After the disciples were faithful to follow Jesus, they were promoted to apostles. Timothy and Titus traveled with Paul helping him as he ministered to the Church; then God promoted them into their own ministries.

Philip, the Evangelist, was called first to be a deacon. He waited on tables. As he was faithful in that ministry, God exalted him into the ministry of an Evangelist.

Sometimes it will appear that a minister is an instant success, but as you look closer, you will see that he was faithful to initially do whatever his hand found to do, and then God exalted him.

The Lord is looking for those who will be faithful in supportive ministries. This is a primary form of service, and if God has anything else for you to do, He will promote you into it as you faithfully serve where you are. Because you are faithful in little things, God can trust you with bigger things.

Be faithful! If you are in a supportive ministry—an assistant, associate pastor, deacon, giver, intercessor, secretary—remember that you are called and anointed by God to fill that position. You are vitally important to the success of that ministry you are serving. As you fulfill that role, God will exalt and promote you in due season.

Everyone has a functional place. *1 Corinthians 12:14* provides: *"For the body is not one member, but many..."* When you read that verse in context, you will see that it is speaking of the gifts of the Spirit. Paul is using the physical body as an illustration; You need all the parts of your body the same way that you need all the gifts of the Spirit to be in operation in the church.

From this illustration, you can see the principle of working together. If we all work together, the job will get done. If we are fussing and fighting among ourselves—competing, crying, and complaining—the job will not get done. If you are not doing your part, you are missing out on what God has in store for you. He will have to move someone else in to take your place. *Your part and function is important*.

God wants you to get involved. Not everyone is called to the front lines. In fact, according to research only one third of all Bible college graduates are called into a senior role. The rest are called into a supportive role.

You may be called into a senior role, but until you get there, you need to be active in a supportive role within the Church. That is where you learn—where you grow. You are in a position of support. God has called you to be involved, to do your share, so that the vision is accomplished. If you are faithful to that calling, God will exalt you.

My first pastor once told me, "You will never be afraid of someone taking your position, if you know God has placed you there. But if you have pushed, shoved, and fought your way into that position, you will always be afraid that someone will push you out and take your position. You will always be one who encourages others and gives them opportunity to serve."

Once you know your place and take it, you will not be upset when God exalts someone else. You will know that your turn is coming! Just keep doing what God has called you to do and you will be exalted.

Take the place God has called you to take and you will be fulfilled and at peace. If you have taken yourself out of position, you can miss what God has in store for you. Just like in any sport, you must be in the proper position to execute the play for the team to score. In like manner, when you are in your position, you help make the Church successful.

James 4:7 states, *"Submit yourselves therefore to God. Resist the devil, and he will flee, (run as if in terror), from you."* The word, 'submit', literally means to find your position in rank. When I am in my position, all the devil can see is Jesus, as I am part of the whole. If I am out of position, he just sees me.

FAITHFULNESS MAKES THE DIFFERENCE

I asked the Lord one time why He had brought me to serve in various ministries and why I was able to have such impact in the area of training people with the Word. His answer shocked me at first. I wanted Him to say it was because of my great teaching ability, or because I was extremely anointed, or because I had so much knowledge. Instead, he said, "I brought you here because I know you will be faithful. You will not only start the job, but you will see the job to completion." He said that because I was faithful; I was chosen.

In *Matthew 20:16* and *22:24* the Scriptures read: "Many are called, but few are chosen." I used to ponder over this portion of Scripture. I knew that God was not a respecter of people, and he would not choose one over another. Therefore, I thought, it had to be something on our part that made the difference between being called and being chosen. The one element that makes the difference is the element of faithfulness.

In *1 Corinthians 4:2* Paul writes: *"Moreover it is required in stewards, that a man be found faithful."* He says that God requires a steward--a minister of His--to be faithful. He did not say you had to be intelligent, be eloquent of speech, or have great natural ability. He said you had to be **_faithful_**. As I studied the Scriptures, I found one outstanding element in the lives of God's men and women: faithfulness.

Over the last 43 years, I have seen many individuals with the call of God upon their lives who are doing nothing for the Lord. When I compared those lives with the ones of those who are working with God, I discovered that the difference was faithfulness (or the lack of it).

Many who were called upon by God were not chosen for His work, because they refused to be faithful. Because of this, they were not promoted into what the Lord had designed for them. Most are sitting around today--waiting to be thrust out into their worldwide teaching and miracle ministry--refusing to do anything less than having top billing and being the one everyone looks to for the answers.

The Scriptures reveal that many are called, but few are chosen. Faithfulness makes the difference. The word *called* means "to be invited or summoned." The word *chosen* means "to be selected." You can see from the definitions that there is a difference between being called and being chosen. You determine the outcome by your faithfulness.

Webster's Dictionary defines *faithful* as "firmly adhering to duty: constant performance of duties; consistent, reliable, dependable." A synonym for faithful is loyal. The word *loyal* is defined as "faithful adherence to a person; faithful to constituted authority; faithful; having an obligation to defend or support."

These two words--*faithful* and *loyal*--may seem insignificant, but they play a major part in the success of failure of your life and ministry. Faithfulness is a character trait--a fruit of the recreated human spirit--that is evidenced throughout the Word of God in reference to men who were successful.

This can be seen readily in the relationship between Paul and Timothy. Timothy was loyal to Paul. In *1 Corinthians 4:7*, Paul describes Timothy as his beloved son and faithful in the Lord. He uses him as an example of loyalty and faithfulness. As a result, Timothy was the only person Paul felt confident to send on important business. He represented Paul and the Lord well.

In dealing with the difference of being called or chosen, it is interesting to look at the life of the apostle Paul. Though he was called to be an apostle in *Acts 9*, it was not until *Acts 13* that Paul was separated for the ministry he had already been called to:

"Separate me Barnabas and Saul (Paul) for the work whereunto I have called them: (Acts 13:2).

It was after this that Barnabas and Paul began their first missionary journey to the provinces of Galatia--a journey that took two years.

When you realize that the time between *Acts 9* and *Acts 13* is 15 years, you can see that Paul did not start out as an apostle. (To compute the time, you use *Galatians 1:18* [3 years], and *Galatians 2:1* [14 years] --a total of 17 years. Subtract the 2 years Paul spent in his first missionary journey. That leaves 15 years between Paul being called and being chosen).

A common misconception is that when called, a person immediately begins to fulfill his ministry. In Paul's life he was faithful as a witness, then as a teacher, then as a prophet for 15 years before he was chosen (separated) for the ministry God had called him to. This time period was a proving time--a time when he was able to make full proof of his ministry

CHAPTER 6   Rewards Of Faithfulness

IMPORTANCE OF FAITHFULNESS

I want to show you another example from the Word that teaches the importance of faithfulness, and the difference between being called and being chosen. This example is seen in the lives and ministries of Elijah and Elisha.

In *1 Kings 19*, Elijah has just come from the slaughter of the prophets of Baal. He has demonstrated that the Lord is the only true God, and Jezebel, King Ahab's wife, wants to kill him for killing all her prophets. Elijah has fled from before her for 40 days. At Mount Horeb, Elijah complains to God that there is no one else that has not bowed to Baal. But, God tells Elijah that there are still 7,000 who have not bowed.

It is in this setting that the Lord tells Elijah what he is to do. He tells Elijah who to anoint as his replacement, "*and Elisha . . . Shall thou anoint to be prophet in thy room*" (*1 Kings 19:16*). The expression "*in thy room*" means in your place. Elijah obeys the Lord and finds Elisha plowing the field with 12 yoke of oxen. Elijah walks by him and casts his mantle upon him. Elisha, immediately knowing what this means, asks the prophet to let him go back and kiss his mother and father.

Elijah's response is designed to have Elisha settle in his own mind the question of his calling.

Elijah says, "Go back again, for what have I done to thee?" (verse 20). Elisha went and slew a yoke of oxen. He burned his bridges behind him, and then *"he arose and went after Elijah and ministered unto him"* (verse 21).

The word "ministered" in Hebrew means, to do menial service or wait on as a servant. Elisha, the next major prophet of Israel, waited on the prophet Elijah. He was his constant companion. He cooked, cleaned, and carried the material Elijah would take with them on a journey. In short, he did all the menial tasks that were at hand to do.

In *2 Kings 2*, we find that the prophet Elijah is going to be taken to heaven, and the mantle is going to fall upon his replacement. The time factor between *1 Kings 19* and *2 Kings 2* is 20 years. Elisha had served this man of God for 20 years. Basically for these 20 years, he had been Elijah's servant. *2 Kings 2:1-15* describes Elisha's succession of Elijah as the prophet in the land. It is important that we see the attitudes of Elisha and those around him, and then see where God places the premium.

This portion of Scripture mentions "the sons of the prophets," referring to schools set up in Israel to teach young men how to respond to the Spirit of God. These schools were located at Bethel and Jericho. When Elijah was going to be taken to heaven, he determined to go to these schools of the prophets. He said to Elisha, *"Tarry here, I pray thee"* (verse 2). But Elisha's response was, *"As the Lord lives and as thy soul lives, I will not leave thee."*

When they arrived at Bethel, the sons of the prophets came to Elisha and began to speak to him. I believe their tone was one of contempt and derision. They were probably "ministering to each other" about who would be the next prophet. They knew Elijah would be taken to heaven, and they looked down on Elisha as just a servant.

It was in this tone that they spoke to Elisha, *"Knowest thou that the Lord will take thy master from the head today?"* (verse 3). In other words, they were saying, "Are you so spiritually ignorant and dumb? Haven't you learned anything these past 20 years? Don't you realize that your master will be taken to heaven today?" Elisha responded, *"Yea I know it; hold ye your peace"* (verse 3). In other words, "Yes, I know it. Why don't you shut up?"

I want us to stop for a moment and consider one other aspect. Though Elisha had served Elijah as a faithful servant for 20 years, there is no record of any miracle Elisha performed or any prophecy he brought forth. There is nothing to indicate that he was to be the next prophet in Israel. This clearly reveals Elisha's faithfulness and loyalty. How many individuals do you know who would wait 20 years for their ministry to come to the forefront?

A DOUBLE PORTION

In *2 Kings 2* we see the rewards and results of faithfulness and loyalty. Elisha would not leave Elijah. His attitude was, "God called me to serve you and be the prophet in your room. I am going to do that until you go to be with the Lord." Together, they crossed over the Jordan on dry ground. They continued to talk, and finally Elijah said: *"Ask what I shall do for thee, before I am taken away from thee."* Elisha said, *"I pray thee, let a double portion of thy spirit be upon me"* (*2 Kings 2:9*).

Now, let me ask you a question. What would have happened if Elisha had not received a double portion of the prophet's spirit? He was called to be Elijah's replacement. He would be the next prophet in the land. If he had not received the double portion, he would still have walked in the same anointing and the same power as Elijah.

Elisha was asking for the right of the first-born male in the household of Israel; a double portion of the inheritance:

"But he shall acknowledge the son of the hated for the firstborn, by giving him a double portion of all that he has; for he is the beginning of his strength; the right of the first born is his." (*Deuteronomy 21:17*).

The concept of the double portion comes from the Law which states that the first born male in a family is entitled to a double portion of the family inheritance. What Elisha is saying is that the relationship between he and Elijah is like that of a father and son. So he is asking for the right of inheritance to a double portion. Do not error, there is not a service where you can come and have hands laid upon you and receive a double portion of the anointing. That is not Scriptural.

In essence, he was saying to Elijah, "You have no wife or children and I have left all. I am like a son unto you. What I want is the right of the first-born son--the double portion."

Elijah's response was, "*Thou hast asked a hard thing: nevertheless, if thou see me when I am taken from thee, it shall be so unto thee; but if not, it shall not be so: (verse 10*). He was saying, 'We will let the Lord make the decision. If you see me being taken up into heaven, it will be as you desired.'

"*And it came to pass as they went on and talked, that behold there appeared a chariot of fire and horses of fire and parted them both asunder; and Elijah went up by a whirlwind into heaven. Elisha saw it and cried; my father, my father, the chariot of Israel and the horsemen thereof: (2 Kings 2:11-12).*

We must remember that no one in the Old Testament ever called God their Father. They were servants of the Lord--not sons and daughters. This is vital in seeing the answer to Elisha's request.

Elijah and Elisha had developed a father/son relationship that gave Elisha the right to ask for a double portion of the inheritance; which was the anointing. He had faithfully served the man of God. Even when he knew he was the next prophet, he did not try to exalt himself or attempt to push his ministry. He served the prophet until it was time for him to be exalted, and then God exalted him.

When Elisha went back to the Jordan River alone, there were 50 of the sons of the prophets standing far away. They wanted to see something, but they were afar off. Elisha wrapped the mantle, smote the water, and walked on dry ground (verse 14). The sons of the prophets then all said, "We know you were the one!"

The double portion Elisha received was in direct relation to his faithfulness. It was given by virtue of relationship and service; like a son with a father. He had a right to the same anointing Elijah had, as he was the one who replaced him. But the relationship that developed between the two, because of Elisha's faithful service, enabled him to ask for and receive a double portion of the anointing. In the ministry of Elijah, seven miracles were recorded. In the ministry of Elisha, 14 miracles are recorded; *double the amount*! Elisha had doubled his ability and effectiveness by his faithful service to the man of God.

I had been invited to hold a teaching seminar in Fresno, California. It was less than one month before we were to move to Oklahoma. I had committed to the meeting, but really did not want to go. Since we were preparing to move to Tulsa, I reasoned that I needed to stay and help my wife get ready for the move.

Every time I prayed about the meeting, the Lord told me to go. I did not want to, but because I had given my word, I went. The main reason I did not want to go was because we had $1,000 in bills, and we needed a new car to help us make the move. I had to become willing and obedient.

When the pastor met me at the airport, the first thing he did was rent a car for me. He then registered me at the Hilton Hotel. As I was getting ready to go to my room, the pastor asked if I needed anything. Though I did not have a dollar in my pocket, I told him I did not need anything. He reached into his pocket and pulled out a wad of bills, gave them to me, and said, "Just in case you see anything you might want." I had never been treated like that before. In most of the places I had ministered, they either put me in the homes of the people in the congregation or in run-down motels. I was praising God!

At the first meeting there were about 50 people present. When the pastor received the offering that night, he said, "The offerings during this seminar are going to Brother Mike's ministry." He then proceeded to receive the evening offering. While he was doing this, the Spirit of the Lord spoke to me and said, "There is a person here who desperately needs a hundred dollars. Take the first hundred dollars from the offering and give it to him." I looked at the size of the crowd and thought, "The first hundred?" It did not look like that much would even come in!

After the offering was received, I asked the pastor, "Did you mean what you said about the offering being mine?" He said, "Yes." So I said to the congregation, "The Lord just spoke to me that someone here is in desperate need of finances, and only one man responded. I said, "Take $100 from the offering and give it to him." I then went back to my seat.

When I sat down, the Lord said to me, "Son there is one thing I required in a steward--he be found faithful. You have been found faithful, and I am going to load it on you." Just to think that the Lord had found me faithful and--as a result--was going to load it on me. What a humbling experience! I began to weep.

The results of that meeting were tremendous. People were healed and the power of the Lord was so strong that some people were unable to stand. There was one little boy, about eight or nine years old, who had one leg shorter than the other, and he had a club foot. He did not know anything about the power of God. His mother had brought him.

The Lord completely healed him. His club foot became normal and his leg grew so that both were the same length.

Financially, the meeting was a success. The offering that came in while I was there was over $800, and an additional $300 came in through the mail while I was in the meetings. That was $1,100, which took care of the needs at home along with the tithe.

The last day a man came up to me and said that the night before, when he and his wife were going to bed, the Lord spoke to them to give me a certain amount personally. It was $1,000. The Lord had said that He was going to load it on me and He did! I came home with enough to not only pay the bills, but to make a down payment on a new station wagon for my family's move to Tulsa. Since that time, God has continued to be true to His promise, and He keeps loading it on.

It is important that you recognize the place faithfulness holds in the things of God. Faithfulness will keep you on the right track. I have never tried to be in the right place at the right time. I have just been faithful to do what was at hand to do, and the Lord has always placed me in the right place at the right time. If you will be faithful, He will do the same for you!

CHAPTER 7   Keeping Clear of Strife

"Now I beseech you, brethren, by the name of our Lord Jesus Christ, that you all speak the same thing, and that there be no divisions among you; but that you be perfectly joined together in the same mind and in the same judgment."(*1 Corinthians 1:10*)

Strife is extremely deadly. *James 3:16* reveals, *"For where envying and strife is, there is confusion [tumult] and every evil work"*. Strife means "rivalry and contention"; but it also means "competition".

If you are competing with another person in the work of the ministry, you are in strife. If you are comparing yourself with another minister or ministry and/or trying to do what they are doing, you are in competition---strife.

I know a man of God who was eating an ice cream cone while watching people ice skate. Suddenly, a young man skated up to him and said, "I know who you are and I know all about your ministry. I just want you to know that my ministry is going to be greater than yours." Once he had said these words, he turned and skated away.

That is competition. The young man was trying to compete with another man of God, and had allowed strife to enter into his heart. If he does don't change his attitude and repent, he is in for big trouble in the future.

I want you to see and an example from the Word that shows how strife can enter in and attempt to destroy a ministry. It happened in Jesus' own ministry.

Matthew 20:20-28 gives us the account of how the mother of James and John asked Jesus if her two sons could sit on either side of Him in His kingdom. The other disciples were moved with indignation. Jesus had to address the situation and straighten out their thinking. He did this by teaching them that the way to greatness is through service. He reminded them that He, Jesus, did not come to be served but to rather serve and give.

THE SNARE OF STRIFE

As I was meditating on this, the Lord began to reveal some things to me. In looking at various Scripture references, we can see that within the twelve disciples, Jesus had an inner circle of three: Peter, James, and John. I believe that the other disciples listened to Satan and became jealous of these three; (even Peter sided with the others when he thought the two most honored positions were going to someone other than himself).

Jesus had to explain to them that he who wanted to be chief among them must be the servant of all. In other words, He was saying that when you get involved helping others get their needs met, God will be able to promote you.

You may remember that when Jesus was on His way to raise Jairus' daughter from the dead, all twelve of the disciples were with Him. But once the woman with the issue of blood was healed, Jesus turned to them and only had Peter, James and John, and Jairus continue on with him. The other nine were left to remained with the multitude, (See *Mark 5:37-42*). These three along with the parents were the only ones Jesus allowed to come with Him into the house.

When Jesus went up to the Mount of Transfiguration, (*Matthew 17:1-8; Mark 9:2-8*), He only took Peter, James and John with Him. The other nine were left at the bottom of the mountain.

I am convinced that the devil used this as an opportunity to sow strife. He most likely whispered to each of them; "Why did He choose them again and not us?"

Notice, if you will that when Jesus came down from the mountain, a man came and asked Him to heal his lunatic son. He had already asked the disciples to heal the boy, but they were unable to do anything.

I believe that one of the reasons the nine could not help the man, was because they had allowed strife to enter their hearts, through envy. I imagine that they had been talking among themselves. I can see them being upset with Peter, James and John, who always seemed to be involved with the most exciting miracles, while they had to stay behind. Their faith was rendered inoperative; and I believe the main reason for this was strife.

The glory of God which was upon that mountain and rested on Jesus was visible for all to see with the naked eye. Just like when Moses came down from Mount Sinai, he did not look the same. Why would it have been different with Peter, James and John after they had been in the glory of God?

Remember, where there is strife, there is confusion and every evil work. The Apostle Paul communicates this even stronger in *2 Timothy 2:22-26.* He says that when you are involved in strive, competing with others, and easily angered, you are taken captive by Satan at his will. In other words, Satan can come in and steal from you any time he wants. Paul also writes that you must recover yourself out of the snare of the devil. God will not recover you until you acknowledge the truth, and then you are able to recover yourself from Satan's snare.

How did Jesus handle strife within His staff, over who would sit next to Him in His kingdom? He used the opportunity to teach them. They listened to Him and were able to recover themselves out of a potential snare. There was no place for Satan to bring division among Jesus' staff.

You may ask; "But how do I recover myself out of the snare of the devil"?

You have to hear the Word and receive it. Then, make the decision that you will not be involved in strife any longer and, turn away from it. As you stand on the Word of God, it will under-gird you. The Spirit of God is there with you and He will put you over.

If you can catch the vision and see how God will use you to help others as he trains and equips you, you will be extremely useful for His work. As you walk in what God calls you to do, you will begin to get a broader scope; you will begin to see more of what the Lord has for you to do.

The unfolding of His will for you may not be exactly what you had thought in the beginning, but you are being molded and formed into an instrument for His use. You will begin to understand that whatever you are doing at this point in time, is what He has designed for you to do; it reality is all about what He determines for your life and ministry, not what you have determined.

I am reminded of a man of God who for ten years, faithfully worked in and supported another man's ministry. He helped other ministries get started and promoted them. Then God promoted him. He pastors a large church and world outreach center. This ministry is not only impacting his state, but are also the nation, as well as helping pastors internationally impact their nations.

God was able to trust him, because he had been faithful to do what was at hand to do in helping others. He was faithful in little, so God gave him authority over much. As he grew in spiritual things, God began to increase his vision and his ability to help others.

God will do the same for you! It may not necessarily be in the same way or in the same time frame, but as you are faithful to what He has called you to do now; He will exalt you in the right time and season.

Always remember:

STEER CLEAR OF STRIFE.

SECTION 2 – *ATTITUDE OF A SERVANT*

CHAPTER 1   The Right Attitude

The attitude you maintain determines the altitude at which you fly. Your attitude determines how high you are going to go, what you are going to do for God, and how successful you will be in the Kingdom of God. *Proverbs 23:7* says; *"For as he thinks in his heart, so is he."*

We've used that verse in referring to faith confessions, "I've got to get the right attitude in my heart. I've got to see myself the way Jesus sees me. The only way I can do that is to view myself through the Word of God." That's true, but there is more to the right attitude than we previously thought. Attitude is the most important thing you will ever have to deal with. It will make you or break you. It will determine success or failure.

The word *attitude* is interesting. Webster's New Collegiate Dictionary defines attitude as "a mental position with regard to a fact or state." In other words, your attitude, or mental position, is produced by certain facts that you have. When you get new facts, therefore, your mental position should change. The "facts" for a Christian are found in the Word of God. When you read the facts in God's Word, your attitude and your mental position should change.

In *Romans 12:1-2,* Paul writes:

"I beseech you therefore, brethren, by the mercies of God, that you present your bodies a living sacrifice, holy, acceptable unto God, which is your reasonable service. And be not conformed to this world, but be transformed by the renewing of your mind, that ye may prove what is the good, and acceptable and perfect will of God."

That first verse is interesting. He said, "I *beseech* you." If you do a word study on *beseech*, you will find that it doesn't mean 'to beg.' It means "to present your case in such a way that it produces the desired results in individuals."

When you beg someone to do something, they might or might not do it. The Greek word translated here as 'beseech" actually means that you present the request in such a way that the other person has no alternative but to do what you've asked. Paul didn't say, "I beg of you to do this. I wish that you would do this." What he did was present his case in such a way that they didn't have a choice.

AN ILLUSTRATION

When I first began a traveling ministry, my family would travel with me. We would go to a hotel at night and my wife would say, "Honey, you don't want to help me get the kids ready for bed, do you?" And she got the answer her question anticipated: "No." Then she got hold of the meaning of the word *beseech* and instead of saying, "You don't want to, do you?" she would say, "Honey, I need some help. Please get the children ready for bed." She was nice and sweet about it, but didn't leave me the choice of saying, "No, I don't want to." My want to, was not involved at all. Now it was, "I need help! Please do it!"

When Paul says, *"I beseech you therefore, brethren, by the mercies of God,"* he is in essence saying: "I am presenting this to you in such a way that you have no alternative but to do it. And the reason you have no alternative is because of all the mercies of God that you have received--salvation, healing, deliverance, baptism of the Holy Spirit, and the gifts of the Spirit. He has given you His life, His nature, and His ability. He has caused you to be prosperous. All things are yours. In view of everything that God has done for you, in view of all the mercies of God, don't you think the least you could do is present your body as a living sacrifice?"

That puts the Scripture in a whole different light. The Amplified Bible helps to show this by stating that presenting your body as a living sacrifice to God *"is your reasonable (rational, intelligent) service and spiritual worship."*

My attitude should be, "God, I'm yours. What do you want me to do? In view of all that you have done for me, what do you want me to do for you?" Paul's words in the next verse make this clearer: *"And be not conformed to this world: but you be transformed by the renewing of our mind."* The word, *transform,* means to go through a complete metamorphosis, a complete change in kind, like the caterpillar that goes into a cocoon and comes out a butterfly.

Basically, Paul is saying, "Do not be conformed to this world. Do not be conformed to the world's standard. Do not be conformed to the external or temporal pressures that come upon you. Be transformed; allow a complete metamorphosis to occur in your life by the renewal of your mind."

The Amplified Bible puts it this way: *"... by the [entire] renewal of your mind by the new ideals and its new attitude."* With a renewed mind--a new attitude; you are going to have a new ideal that sets a standard, a goal, and a vision in front of you of what you need do and be.

NEW ATTITUDE AND NEW IDEALS

Your new attitude and new ideals will be determined by God. The reason is that your mind has been renewed by the Word of God. The word *attitude* also means a position in relationship to a fixed point of reference. That was something I understand because I'm a pilot and loved to fly. Flying can teach you some very important lessons.

In the airplane, there is an instrument with an artificial horizon. It shows a little airplane, the sky, and the ground. If you become enveloped in a cloud bank or lose visibility some other way, you must trust and believe what that instrument shows you. If not, you may think you are going in one direction when you are really going in another. You may think you are in a climbing turn to the left when you actually descending to the right.

That instrument tells you whether you are going up or down; level or banking to the left or to the right. Even when all your senses tell you something else, you need to trust and believe the instrument--it shows your position in relationship to your only fixed point of reference--the ground.

The Word of God is our instrument that shows us a fixed point of reference and our relationship to it. Your attitude is your position in relation to that fixed point of reference. Your attitude will determine your actions.

When I first began to study the attitude of a servant, I saw that the emphasis was on service, holiness, effectiveness, and purity of motive. The Lord showed me times in my life when I had opportunities to exhibit this attitude, and times when I had not.

Years ago, I worked with the Los Angeles Police Department as a Chaplain for five and a half years. I didn't work in the prisons. I worked on the front lines in patrol cars dealing with barricaded suspects, with hostages, with attempted suicides, or in family disputes--all the easy things!

After I'd been on the job for a year, I saw a need in the department for a set of uniform guidelines that could be followed by all our Chaplains. I wrote down my suggestions and presented them to one of the Commanders. He was nice and took me to lunch. In other words, he humored me. But he said my suggestions were not needed.

About two years later, we had a day-long meeting with all the LAPD Chaplains. We were divided into groups for discussions and to give our opinions as to what direction we thought the program should take. Each group presented their recommendations to the Commander. He then prepared his report. The Commander's findings were exactly what I had presented to him two years prior. He only made minor adjustments to what I had originally presented to him. He then presented it as a comprehensive program for the Chaplain Corps. It had become his project.

I did not become upset, but I praised God because what I saw as a great need was going to be implemented. When you begin to deal with effectiveness and motives and your attitude is one of service, it doesn't matter who gets the credit. Your concern is that the needs are going to be met.

Later, I worked on developing a curriculum for a Bible Institute. When it was completed, it was taken and used overseas. The introductory page highlighted the curriculum and the school, and it included a picture of the staff. There was, however, no picture or mention of me--even though I had created and written the entire curriculum. My attitude was, "God, I get credit with you, and the main thing is that it's being used and that people's lives are going to be changed. That is what's important."

CONCEIT OR SELF-ESTEEM

Now it's good to have a strong sense of identity. In fact, if you don't have a healthy self-esteem, you probably won't be very productive in the Kingdom of God. You need to have a strong spirit that says, "You can do it, you can do it, you can do it." But you need to keep your ego--all the self things, in-line with the Word; proclaiming, "I can do it, because I can do all things through Christ who strengthens me." This keeps you in the proper perspective compared to the Lord (see *Philippians 4:13*). "I can do it because of Christ. I can do it--and praise God, look at what I have done."

Some may say, "Brother, I wouldn't talk like that." But in *Matthew 25*, the Parable of the Talents tells us that when the master reckoned with the servant, his answer was, "Lord, this is what I have done with what you have given me." He didn't say, "I didn't do anything." He said "You gave this to me and I took it and produced twice as much." He recognized that it came from his Master, that it had been entrusted to him, and that he had something to do with producing the result. You must have confidence in yourself.

After the Lord showed me this, I went to my pastor and said, "Pastor, I have just discovered that I have a really big ego. But I have learned to determine what is me and what is God, and I know how to keep my ego in check." He said, "That's good--because if you didn't have a large ego, you wouldn't be of any benefit or value to me." That's the difference between people who are self-motivated, and people who must have supervisors constantly telling them what to do. People who are self-motivated have a strong sense of identity. They know who they are.

Romans 12:3 says: "For I say, through the grace given to me, to every man that is among you, not to think of himself more highly that he ought to think."

That is why it's so important to understand the **Attitude of a Servant**. Once you have developed this attitude, ego is no longer a problem. The **Attitude of a Servant** keeps pride and self-will from arising, and keeps self in its proper place.

CHAPTER 2   Saved to Serve

RECREATED TO WORK

Ephesians 6:5-8 says:

"Servants, be obedient to them that are your masters according to the flesh, with fear and trembling, in the singleness of your heart, as unto Christ; Not with eye service, as men pleasers; but as the servants of Christ, doing the will of God from the heart; With good will doing service, as to the Lord, and not to men: Knowing that whatsoever good thing any man doeth, the same shall he receive of the Lord, whether he be bond or free."

The Amplified Bible translates *"in singleness of your heart"* as *"in singleness of motive."* You should write that in the margin of your Bible. The next verse in The Amplified Bible says, *"Not in the way of eye service, as if they were watching you, and only to please men; but as servants (slaves) of Christ, doing the will of God heartily and with your whole soul."* This is because "in singleness of motive" and "doing the will of God with your whole soul" --both of these depict attitudes.

It is God's will that we serve. It is God's will that we work. Adam was created in the image and likeness of God. When Adam fell, a void was formed on the inside of man that can only be filled when he comes back into relationship with God.

When you come back into this relationship, you are recreated.

RECOGNIZE YOUR PURPOSE

There's a God-shaped void on the inside of each and every person, and it can only be filled when you're born again. Once you are born again, and filled with the Spirit, you are just aglow with the presence of God. But you will notice that after a period of time, if you are not serving, a void seems to develop. You become just as miserable as you were before becoming recreated. Why; because you have been saved (born again) to serve. You notice that something is missing; you do not seem to know what it is. Why has that void come back; what is wrong?

Receiving Jesus did fill that God-shaped void. But, once that empty space was filled and you do not go on to become a servant, you will find a new void developing. God called us to serve. We are recreated *"in Christ Jesus unto good works."* If I do not work (serve), there will be a void and I will become miserable.

Ephesians 2:8-10 (KJV)

"For by grace are you saved, through faith; and that not of yourselves: it is the gift of God; Not of works, lest anyone should boast; For we are his workmanship, created in Christ Jesus unto good

works, which God has before ordained that we should walk in them:"

<u>*The Message Bible translates verse 10;*</u>

"He creates each of us by Christ Jesus to join Him in the works he does; the good works He has gotten ready for us; work we had better be doing."

In reading this portion of Scripture, something caught my attention. It is the fact that we are **saved for a purpose**. God did not just save us to take us to heaven, or that he wanted someone else to fellowship with. He saved us with a purpose (destiny) in mind. God did not save you to take you to heaven. Now before you get upset, I did not say that you are not going to heaven. I said that the purpose of your salvation is not to provide you with fire insurance to escape Hell's fire.

Heaven is a by-product of this salvation experience. You cannot go to heaven unless you are saved, but it is not the main reason behind your salvation. It is like water. You cannot jump in a swimming pool without getting wet, but you do not say I am going to jump in pool of wet. By the same token, when you ask for a glass of water, you do not ask for a glass of wet.

Wet is a by product of coming in contact with water which is the chemical compound to H_2O. This is manifested in three forms: Solid (ice), Gaseous (steam), and Liquid (water). Each three is the same chemical make up and the result of contact with it produces wetness.

It is the same with our salvation. We are saved for a purpose, and that purpose is to serve. If I am not serving, I am not doing what I was saved for.

KEEPING IT IN PERSPECTIVE

In *Ephesians 6:6* Paul says, *"Doing the will of God from your heart."* You are to work with singleness of motive, doing the will of God. "Well," you say. "What is the will of God?" WORK! "Why?; Because *you are recreated "in Christ Jesus unto good works."* You are recreated in Christ to work.

When I saw that, it put some things into perspective for me. I am recreated to work. *"Knowing that whatsoever good thing any man doeth, the same shall he receive from the Lord, whether he be bond or free"* (*Ephesians 6:8*). Paul is saying do the will of God with singleness of heart because when you do, you will be rewarded by God.

GOD USE ME

The heart cry of every believer is for God to use them. They pray, God use me, and really want to be in the will of God. This is admirable but in many instances this is prayed, without understanding of what we are asking and what the Scripture teaches.

Isaiah 33:6 (a)

"And wisdom and knowledge shall be the stability of your times, and the strength of salvation;"

Psalms 119:130

"The entrance of thy word gives light; it gives understanding to the simple."

Proverbs 2:6-7

"For the Lord gives wisdom: out of his mouth comes knowledge and understanding;

He lays up sound wisdom for the righteous; he is a buckler to them that walk uprightly."

We want to be used by God but we are afraid of doing the wrong thing, so we wind up doing nothing. We want to make sure that we are in the perfect will of God, so we hesitate and do nothing.

We have been erroneously taught that *Romans 12:2* tells us God has three wills: the acceptable will; the good will; and the perfect will. This is not true. The words acceptable, good and perfect are adjectives. An adjective in the English language is a word that is used to define a noun (subject). It is not a listing of different things, but words that are used to define that one thing.

There is only one will of God. Either you are in it or you are not. His will is acceptable, good and perfect. His will is for you to serve (work). So we can answer the question of what is God's will for me by stating that His will is for you to serve in whatever capacity is opened to you.

Romans 6:18, 22

"Being then made free from sin, you became servants of righteousness."

"But now being made free from sin, and become servants to God, you have your fruit unto holiness, and the end everlasting life."

Titus 2:14

"Who gave himself for us, that he might redeem us from all iniquity, and purify unto himself a peculiar people, ZEALOUS of good works."

A vast majority of people in our churches have a heart to do something for God, but do not know where to start. They want to ***feel led***. This is a term we use to absolve ourselves from doing something we do not want to do. When an opportunity is presented to work as an usher, or in the nursery, or in the children's ministry, our response is that we do not ***feel led***. Let me shatter that excuse, because that is all it is, an excuse wrapped up in "spiritual language".

We continue to seek God and ask him to use us, but every time there is an opportunity, we do not feel it is for us. We say something like, 'Lord speak to whoever it is that is supposed to be doing this.'

Finally the Pastor asked you individually to take this position or take on this service. We respond with what I call the 'Great Christian Lie' .... "I'll pray about it." Every pastor knows when a congregant says this to them, that they will not be accepting this opportunity but blaming it on God, for their inaction.

But I am convinced better of you. I know that if you are asked to do serve in an area, and you respond with I'll pray about it...you will actually pray about it. But unfortunately you will pray like I did before I was saved.

MY ENCOUNTER

I was approached by a group of Mormon missionaries, who had received my name from an individual I had known. They came to my fraternity house, looking for me. After introductions, they proceeded to "share" with me what they felt was the truth. I informed them that I was Jewish, and they said that is good, as you then have a greater understanding of what we are sharing with you.

They finally asked me to simply pray, and in fact instructed me to pray asking the God of Abraham, Isaac, and Jacob, whether Mormonism is right. I told them that I would...and I did. I prayed just like many in the church do, when they are asked to serve.

I prayed, "O God; God of Abraham, Isaac, and Jacob. I thank you that Judaism is right and Mormonism is wrong...Amen."

The missionaries contacted me the next week and asked me if I had prayed. I assured them I had, and they proceeded to let me know when my baptism was going to be set for. I informed them that I was not going to be baptized. This led to a back and forth discussion. In exasperation they finally asked, what God said when I prayed. I told them that God had said Judaism was right and Mormonism was wrong. They left me alone after that and to this day I have never been contacted again by Mormon missionaries.

You are asking, what this has to do with me...everything. When you say you will pray about it, you pray like this:

'Father, I thank you that the pastor is finally recognizing your hand upon me, and can see that you desire to use me; BUT thank you that this area of service is not your will for me.'

You then proceed to inform the pastor that you have prayed, and God let you know that this is not what He has for you to do. You have just spoken an untruth and demonstrated you do not know the Scriptures.

You should be honest and say; Pastor unless it is to teach, preach, heal the sick, raise the dead, cast out devils, or take over the adult Sunday school class; it is not for me.

WHAT IS GOD'S WILL?

It is not hard to determine what God's will for you to do is. In fact, I will let you know what it is without prophesying. His will is to do whatever your hand finds to do.

Ecclesiastes 9:10

"Whatsoever your hand finds to do, do it with your might; for there is no work, nor device, not knowledge, nor wisdom, in the grave where you are headed."

Is there anything that does not fall into the category of whatsoever? NO! You are whosoever, so you are to do whatsoever; because where you are headed there is no place of service to perform. If you are not doing anything, and an opportunity for service arises...that is the Will of God for you.

If you are supposed to be doing something else, your service, where you are at, will bring you to the attention of the people who have need of your gift. It is very easy to steer a moving vehicle, but impossible to steer a vehicle that is parked.

In *Proverbs 18:16*, we read, *"A man's gift makes room for him, and brings him before great men."* If you are called of God, your gift will make room for you. Your responsibility now is to help in any capacity you can, and let God exalt you. You can readily see from a study of the Word that men of God who were exalted into prominent ministers did not start there. They began by doing what was at hand; then God exalted them.

The apostles did not begin as apostles. They were disciples first. They began by doing the menial tasks, as we have already seen. Then, in the Book of Acts we saw how these same men were exalted to the office of apostle. They were giving themselves to the Word of God and to prayer. God exalted them!

The most important element to your success in any ministry is to know beyond a shadow of doubt that you are called of God. No matter what you are called to do – whether it is to fill one of the five-fold ministries or to be a deacon, a hostess, or a maintenance man – you must realize that you are called of God.

So often, people think that to be called of God, they must be in full-time ministry or occupy an office of ministry such as prophet or evangelist. That is not true. **You are called of God to support the work of the Gospel with your prayers, your tithes and offerings, your time, and your talents.** You are called just as much as the individual in a five-fold gift ministry. In fact, if you let down on your responsibility, the work of God could suffer.

There is a place in the Body of Christ for each of us. If you do not fulfill your calling, there will be a weak link in the chain – an open spot in the armor. Some people say, "Unless I can be in front of everyone, I am useless to God." That is a lie from the devil! You are just as valuable behind the ministry–praying, confessing the Word, and loving those in the ministry.

I have seen teenagers take hold of this and begin to move out for God. Some of them surpass even the adults in spiritual maturity as they do whatever is set before them. Let me give you an example of this.

In the reception area of one particular church, there was a planter containing plastic flowers – the kind that look really fake. As people walked by, they would say, "Those plastic flowers look horrible! Why doesn't someone do something about it?"

The church staff wanted to replace them, but nobody seemed to have the time. One day a teenage girl came in and said, "You know, I've been thinking of planting real plants in the church reception area. Would that be okay?" The adults didn't have the time, but a teenager did. She knew her calling!

Paul knew his calling. In *Romans 1:1 and I Corinthians 1*, he states his calling: *Paul, called to be an apostle...*He had no doubt about it! But Paul didn't begin in the office of apostle. It was seventeen years from the time he was called to be an apostle until the time he was thrust out in that office (*Acts 9; 13; Galatians 1; 2*). The rest of that time, Paul was simply teaching and preaching, helping out wherever he could.

Though he was not walking in the office of an apostle, he knew he was called. It took time to develop his ministry. Paul was a teacher and a prophet; then after being found faithful, he was exalted to the office of apostle and sent out by the Holy Spirit.

I want you to realize that it takes time to get from "Point A" to "Point B." You don't enter kindergarten one week and find yourself in college the next week. There are certain types of schools where a student can progress at his own pace and move up as rapidly as he wants. If he is capable of doing the work and has the determination and drive to do it, he can graduate from high school at age 16.

REWARDS FROM GOD

Your reward does not come from man, but from God. So when you are working and serving with singleness of motive, whether you get any recognition from man doesn't matter. Whatever you do, you will receive the same of the Lord.

My two oldest children, Michael and Linda, experienced a personal example of this when they were very young. They had accompanied my wife and me on a ministry trip to Holland and Norway.

During our time in Holland, the children decided to help out with the work in the mission's tape room. They put labels on tapes, filled tape holders, and cataloged tapes. They were so excited about serving the Lord that they did not view it as work. In fact, we had to make them sit down and eat their meals. They wanted to just grab a quick bite and get back to work. They were doing this on a voluntary basis, asking no pay nor expecting any. They were doing it out of a love for the Lord.

One night I told them, "The Lord will reward you for your labor of love for His name." I reminded them of *Luke 6:38, "Give and it shall be given unto you."* They were not working for a reward, but God rewards the faithful (*Ephesians 6:8, Proverbs 28:20*).

On our last day in Holland, my wife Martha went to the market place to buy some food, clothes, and toys. While she was there, a woman approached her and said, "I have been in Bible school this week and have been so blessed by your husband's ministry. I just bought these gifts for your children." With that, she handed Martha a large bag filled with gifts for the children.

Martha brought the gifts back, and that evening we gave them to the children. Michael's first comment was, "See, Linda, Daddy told us God would bless us for serving Him." He realized that the gifts really were from God for their service to Him. They not only received satisfaction from a job well done, but received a reward in this world as well. Service with the right motive produces for the Kingdom of God and for you.

This same principle applies with God. You can move as rapidly as you desire with God but it requires study and meditation in God's Word, then corresponding action.

CHAPTER 3   The Mind of Christ

LET THIS MIND BE IN YOU

There's a familiar passage of Scripture in *Philippians 2:5* that we haven't understood clearly in the past: *"Let this mind be in you, which was also in Christ Jesus."* That means you should let the mind, the thoughts, the attitudes, and the ideals--the standard that was in Christ Jesus--be in you. Glory to God!

The *sixth verse* continues: *"Who, being in the form of God, thought it not robbery to be equal with God."* We have heard this preached and have become excited about it. We have said, "Praise God, the mind of Christ is in me. I do hold the thoughts, the intents, and the purposes of God's heart. I have the mind of Christ."

We have also said, "I have the mind of Christ. I don't think it's robbery to be equal with God because I am a joint heir with Jesus." We have used that, among other verses, to prove that we have been made *"the righteousness of God"* (*2 Corinthians 5:21*). And this is as far as we went. *Psalm 82:6* says: *"I have said, you are gods; and all of you are children of the most High.* But that's god with a lower case "g." We were created in the image of God to rule and reign in this earth. And then we were recreated in Christ Jesus.

He *"thought it not robbery to be equal with God."* We are equal with God in the sense that we're joint heirs with Jesus Christ. Because of your position in Him, we are equal with Jesus in that aspect.

But we skipped verses 7 and 8 of Philippians chapter 2 and went on to verses 9 and 10, which say; *"Wherefore God also has highly exalted him, and given him a name which is above every name. That at the name of Jesus every knee should bow ..."* We said, "God has highly exalted me and given me a name that is above every name. I have the name of Jesus. Everything must bow to the name of Jesus."

The verses we ignored however, give the proper context for all this: *"But made himself of no reputation, and took upon him the form of a servant, and was made in the likeness of men: And being found in fashion as a man, he humbled himself and became obedient unto death, even the death of the cross"* (*Philippians 2:7-8*).

Paul is saying that because of our position in Christ, we should make ourselves of no reputation. He is not saying we should exalt ourselves. The highly exalted part didn't come until after the humbling and obedience.

In *Matthew 20:28* Jesus says,

"Even as the Son of man came not to be ministered unto, but to minister." If He had wanted to be ministered to, He would have remained in heaven. But He came to minister and so He made Himself "of no reputation." You cannot make yourself "nothing" until you have been "something." Jesus was not concerned about anything. He was satisfied. He knew who He was, what He was to do and therefore, didn't need to make a reputation for Himself.

People who need to make a reputation for themselves, and to make their name known are insecure. Jesus was secure. When you are secure, you can make yourself of no reputation. If you are insecure, you have to have a reputation. Jesus humbled Himself by being obedient. The best way for us to be humble is to learn to be obedient.

I come from a family of five children. We all had various chores to do around the house. When I was 16, I decided that housework was "women's work." I told this to my dad. I thought that now I was a man and didn't need to scrub floors or wash windows or do any other type of "women's work." I was in for a rude awakening. My dad let me know in no uncertain terms that helping around the house was not "women's work."

He told me all of the chores were done by the family working together to achieve a common goal. He made a statement that had a lasting impact on my spirit. He said, "If doing so called 'women's work' makes you feel less of a man, then you're in trouble. You are insecure inside yourself and in your masculinity."

That statement is so true. If you are secure within yourself, what you do or how you function doesn't determine who you are. We are to be totally identified with Christ. Because of that, it doesn't matter what job we do for Him.

One time we had a Prophet that ministered to our church staff. When he came to me he said to me; "Be humble; be humble; be humble." So I started examining my life. I talked with him afterwards and he said, "The Lord wasn't displeased--He was just giving you advice for the future."

A few months later he returned to the church and brought up the subject again. He singled me out and said, "The Lord was not displeased with you or telling you that you were not humble. He was just reminding you to stay that way." So I told God, "You know I want to stay humble and obedient. I don't want false humility, nor do I want to walk below my rights and privileges. I want to walk fully in what God has provided for me." As long as we have the mind of Christ in this way--by being humble and obedient--we can serve Him in the way He wants us to and do all He has for us. In this mindset, we are poised to use all our talents and abilities to their fullest.

.

CHAPTER 4   The Parable of the Talents

While I was studying the Word of God one day, a portion of Scripture seemed to stand out. In it I found God's plan for doubling our ability and productivity in the kingdom of God. That portion of Scripture is *Matthew 25:14-30 (KJV).* It reads:

"For the kingdom of heaven is as a man traveling into a far country, who called his own servants, and delivered unto them his goods. And unto one he gave five talents, to another two and another one; to every man; according to his own personal ability; and straightway took his journey.

The that had received the five talents went and traded with the same and made them another five talents. And likewise he that had received two, he also gained other two. But he that had received one went and dug in the earth and hid his lord's money. After a long time, the lord of those servants cometh and reckoned with them.

And so he that had received five talents came and brought other five talents, saying, 'Lord, thou delivered unto me five talents: behold, I have gained beside them five talents more.' His lord said unto him, 'Well done, thy good and faithful servant: thou hast been faithful over a few things, I will make thee ruler over many things; enter thou into the joy of thy lord. 'He also that had received two talents came and said, 'Lord, thou delivered unto me two talents: behold, I have gained two other talents beside them.' His lord said unto him, 'Well done, good and faithful servant; thou hast been faithful over few things, I will make thee ruler over many things; enter thou into the joy of the lord. 'Then he which had received the one talent came and said, 'Lord, I knew thee that thou art a hard man, reaping where you have not sown and gathering where you have not strawed:

And I was afraid and went and hid thy talent in the earth: lo, there thou hast that is yours' His lord answered and said unto him, 'Thou wicked and slothful servant, thou knew that I reap where I sowed not and gather where I have not strawed: Thou should therefore to have put my money to the exchangers and then at my coming I should have received mine own with usury. Take therefore the talent from him and give it unto him which hath ten talents. For unto every one that hath shall be given and he shall have abundance: but from him that hath not shall be taken away even that which he has. And cast ye the unprofitable servant into outer darkness: there shall be weeping and gnashing of teeth.' Matthew 25:14-30 (KJV)

Many who read this parable have a preconceived idea concerning the talents. They think the talents still belonged to the master after he had given them to his servants. This is not so, and such thinking will prejudice our under-standing of this parable. It is important that we let the Word speak for itself.

THE KINGDOM

In this parable, Jesus is teaching His disciples (and us) how to double their ability in the kingdom of heaven. The term *kingdom of heaven* or *kingdom of God* has a very definite meaning in the Scriptures. It refers to our living in the totality of the rule of the Lord upon this earth. When Jesus taught about the kingdom, He was teaching how to operate in the principles that govern the operation of the sphere of God's dominion and rule (*see Matthew 16:19; 18:18; Ephesians 2:6*).

The word '*kingdom*' carries two distinct meanings when used in the New Testament. Firstly; "*the sphere of dominion*" and secondly: "*the activity of reigning.*" This second meaning, "*the activity of reigning*," carries three basic elements: (1) bringing deliverance, (2) conferring blessings, and (3) exercising authority.

When we understand that the kingdom of heaven is the activity of reigning, then we can better understand the parables of Jesus. When He is teaching that the kingdom of heaven is like unto, He is telling us that this parable will teach us how to operate in the activity of reigning.

In the above passage from Matthew's Gospel, we can see that Jesus is instructing His disciples on how to operate in the activity of reigning. By taking this portion of Scripture and examining it piece by piece, we can see how to operate in the kingdom of heaven. In verse 14 we read, "... *and delivered unto them his goods.*"

Notice the word "delivered." It means "to deliver over, to surrender, and to yield up." It is the same word used in *Romans 8:32* when speaking of God delivering up His Son for us. When something (or someone) is delivered, it becomes the property of the one to whom it is delivered. Jesus was delivered up for us. He is ours and we are His. This can also be seen in *Ephesians 5:25*, where the word "gave" is the same word as translated "delivered" in *Matthew 25*.

In our text, verse 15 tells us that the goods were portioned out to the servants. One man received five, one received two, and one received one. According to this verse in The Amplified Bible, each man was given "in proportion to his own personal ability."

TALENT

A *talent* is a monetary measurement, which today is approximately the equivalent of $1,000. That would be a fortune in Jesus day, as the average wage was a penny per day, (a penny being worth 15 cents). The average worker earned $54.75 a year, which was considered a livable wage.

In this relation, you can see that the master delivered a small fortune to each of his servants. The first man was given $5,000, the second man,

$2,000, and the third man, $1,000. Each man was given in proportion to his own personal ability to use it--no more and no less.

It is important to understand that each man had the ability to use what was delivered to him. They were not asked to go beyond their ability, but to operate within the scope of the ability they had.

Have you ever been asked to become involved with some aspect of your church? You might have been asked to serve as host or hostess, counselor, usher, or maybe even teacher of the toddler's class. You were not being asked to do a job held by someone else, but rather to do something for the kingdom of God according to the ability you have.

In another rendering of this parable, *Luke 19:12-26*, we can find further clarification of this principle. *Luke 19:13* reads: "*Delivered unto them ten pounds and said unto them, occupy until I come.*" The word "occupy" means "to enter into transaction; to do business; to trade; to enter into commerce." In other words, each man was given the talents (money) to enter into commerce according to his ability.

When each man received the talents, they became his. They were no longer the master's; they became the servant's. We have looked at this parable religiously and thought the master demanded the talents and the increase from each man when he reckoned with them. This is not so.

They were no longer the master's once he gave them to the servants.

In *Matthew 25:16-18* we see what each individual did with the money he had received. The man who had received the five talents ($5,000) traded with the same. He entered into commerce and made an additional $5,000. The man who had received the two talents ($2,000) did the same and he gained another $2.000. The man who received the one talent ($1,000) hid his lord's money in the earth.

Then the master of the servants returned and reckoned with them (verse 19). This is where we tend to become bogged down with traditional thinking. Most think that when the lord reckoned with his servants, he wanted both his money and the money they had gained. That is not so.

According to Webster's 20th Century Unabridged Dictionary, the word 'reckon' means "to explain, to tell, to make a reckoning." The word reckoning means "a settlement of rewards; a measuring of possibilities for the future."

That brings the meaning of this point of the parable into a clearer focus. The master had quite a lot held in reserve for these servants, but they were given an initial amount to see how they would perform. **The blessings of the future are built upon the faithful and consistent use of what you have now.** Your future will be determined by how you use what is currently in your hand. The life you have now is a direct result of the choices you have made, and the use of what has been entrusted into your hands.

Here in *Matthew 25* the master of these servants was asking for an accounting of what the men had done with a view to future plans and possibilities. He was not asking for the money (talents). He just wanted to know what the men had done with the money, so he could reward them for their faithfulness.

I want you to notice the attitude among these servants. Each man was given according to his own personal ability. The first two men had the same attitude when they reckoned with the master. Both said, *"You delivered unto me and I have gained."* Both had received the money as their own and were relating what they had done with it--what they had accomplished.

A PROPER ATTITUDE

The attitude of some believers today is one of false humility. They say, "Brother, I would never say 'I have done something.' It was God, and I wouldn't want to share His glory." This sounds good and seems right, but it is a subtle form of deception. It is true that without God we could do nothing, but we are not without Him. We *"can do all things through Christ who strengthens us"* (Philippians 4:13).

We are accountable for what we do with the abilities God has given us. We are to boldly say, "You have given to me and I have done this with it." This attitude is pleasing to God. Remember, the parable in *Matthew 25* is teaching us how to operate in the kingdom of God.

The Lord did not rebuke these men and say they were egotistical and boastful. He did not punish them for having a prideful attitude. He said, in essence, "Well done, you good and faithful servant. You are to be commended for using what I gave you to the best of your ability. You have been faithful over a few things; I will make you ruler over many things. Enter into the joy of your lord."

Now let us look at the attitude of the third servant. This man dug a hole in the earth and hid his lord's money (*Matthew 25:18*). But, it was not his lord's money, it was his. The money had been delivered to him. He displayed a very poor attitude that became even more pronounced when the master asked for an accounting.

"Then he which had received the one talent came and said, lord, I know thee that thou art a hard man; reaping where thou hast not sown and gathering where thou hast not strawed: And I was afraid and went and hid thy talent in the earth: lo, there thou hast what is thine" (Matthew 25:24-25).

This servant displayed an attitude of fear, which will cause either inaction or improper action. The servant said, "I know you are a hard man. I was afraid of you, so I went and hid your money. Here, you can have your money back."

A quick look at this and at the master's response would lead one to think that the master had been demanding his money back. In actuality, the master was responding to the servant in the manner he had been spoken to. The master said:

"Thou wicked and slothful servant . . . Thou should have therefore to have put my money to the exchangers and then at my coming I should have received mine own with usury [interest]" (Matthew 25:26-27).

We can have a clearer understanding of what is taking place by looking at *Luke 19:22.* This verse says: *"And he saith unto him, **out of your own mouth will I judge thee.**"* The lord responded in a manner that had been predetermined by the attitude and words of the servant.

Proverbs 18:20 says, "A man's belly shall be satisfied with the fruit of his mouth." The Word also teaches that we have to eat the fruit produced by the words we speak.

The master was dealing with the third servant on the basis of the servant's attitude, as expressed in his words. The master said, in essence, 'Since you said this is my money, I will judge you that way. You are lazy, wicked, slothful, and of no use. If the money were mine, you should have at least put it in the bank to draw interest. Then I would have had my money with interest.'

I want to stress that the master was not saying the money was his. He had delivered it to the servant. The servant determined how he would be judged--by his attitude, his words, and his actions. I believe that if the man had taken the $1,000; entered into business and lost it all, the master would have said, "Well done, thou good and faithful servant." At least the man would have been doing something with what had been given to him.

DON'T WASTE YOUR TALENTS

Many of God's people have talents and abilities that are not being used, because they are waiting for God to do something. God has given you talents and abilities. He expects you to put them to use.

If you are not busy for the kingdom of God (and I am not talking about full-time ministry), you are slothful and lazy. God never called people to be pew sitters. There is no such office in the New Testament! God has placed you in a church or ministry that needs your talent and ability to help supply all that is necessary for that ministry (*1 Corinthians 12:18*).

We see the same truth in *Ephesians 4:16*. Speaking of the Church, the Apostle Paul said: "*The whole body fitly joined together and compacted by that which every joint supplies, according to the effectual working in the measure of every part, makes increase of the body unto the edifying of itself in love."* We need each other to get the job done, so put your talent to work and begin producing for the kingdom of God.

USE WHAT YOU HAVE

Let us examine the two faithful servants and see not only their attitude but also their productivity. Each man was given according to the ability he had.

In *Matthew 25:20-23* we saw how the first two servants took the money that had been given them and entered into commerce. They used the money and let it produce for them. Both men doubled the original amount they had been given. The man with $5,000 entered into business and used his ability to double his original sum. The man who had received $2,000 did the same. He used his money to the best of his ability, and it doubled for him.

Now notice that each man was given according to his several abilities. Not only did these men double their money, they doubled their ability. The man who accumulated a total of $10,000 also gained the ability to use that much. The man who accumulated a total of $4,000 likewise also gained the ability to use that much. There is a principle of operating in life, no matter what you do. If you use what you have to the best of your ability, you will not only double your productivity; you will also double your ability.

This is a continuous progression. The man who received the $2,000 and doubled it has a concept working for him. He then had $4,000 and the ability to use that amount. If he continued to use his money to the best of his ability, he would continue to double both his money and his ability. Think of that! He started with 2 and then had 4. Next he would have had 8, then 16, then 32, then 64, then 128 and so on.

STEPPING UP TO A HIGHER LEVEL

Can you see the importance of using your talents to the utmost of your ability? You will not only double your productivity, you will double your ability.

We stated earlier that the parables about the kingdom were written to give us the example of how to operate in the kingdom of God. Your effectiveness will be governed by your use of what the Lord has given to you.

The Apostle Paul states in *1 Corinthians 2:6 (Amplified Bible): "Yet when we are among the full-grown--spiritually mature Christians who are ripe in understanding--we do impart a (higher) wisdom [that is, the knowledge of the divine plan previously hidden]."* This implies that there is something not readily available without some prior knowledge.

In your Christian walk, certain things become clearer as you grow. It must be line upon line, precept upon precept. You are always building upon what you have already learned.

The kingdom of God--the activity of reigning--operates the same way. As you become proficient in one area, you move to the next higher level of proficiency. Once you realize that Jesus is the Healer, you pray for the sick and begin to see results. The more results you have, the greater the degree of accuracy and boldness on your part. But if you never begin, you will never operate in that kingdom principle.

IT WORKED FOR ME!

I would like to share some personal experiences that will act as windows for you to see this principle of doubling your ability in operation. We learn by both precept and example.

When I was the assistant pastor of a church in southern California, my responsibilities included preaching once a week in the main service, preaching when the senior pastor was out of town, overseeing the Sunday school department, and making sure the ushers knew their functions. After being on staff for about four months, I was asked by the pastor to take over the Bible school. The school was in trouble financially and numerous students were dropping out.

God had given the pastor a vision to train and equip men and women for the ministry with the accurate Word of God. The only way that church knew to do this was by starting a Bible school. One of the classes was a survey of the Old Testament. In a twelve-week period, the students had to read and outline the entire Old Testament besides learning the kings and prophets of both the Northern and Southern Kingdoms of Israel. This was quite a bit for the students to do in addition to their other classes. Many of them had not been in school for years.

While talking with the pastor, I suggested that in view of the vision God had given him, he needed a training center rather than a Bible school. He agreed, and then asked me to take charge.

I thought, "God, You never called me to run a Bible training center. You called me to teach and preach." This was an attitude I had to deal with. I had no desire to do it and did not think I had the necessary ability. But the ability had to be in me, or the Spirit of God would never have prompted the pastor to ask me to run this important facet of his ministry. I had to begin by faith. I could easily have said I was not called to start a Bible training center. Instead, I trusted the Lord and relied on Him for wisdom and guidance.

To transform the school into a training center, it was necessary to develop a curriculum, set a fee structure, design advertising material, and form a schedule of classes. By spending time in prayer, I was given direction from the Lord. The result was a nine-month, four-hour-per-week course taught on Saturdays. It consisted of three twelve-week semesters with four classes taught each semester. The first year we graduated 27 students. The second year we enrolled 220 students and graduated 200.

The success of the school did two things: it trained men and women in the Word and out working for the Lord and, it produced $40,000 for the church in a nine-month period. I soon learned about the increase in my productivity and my ability.

The initial curriculum (12 classes) was being used successfully, and I was extremely happy. I supposed that there would be no need to do anything else with curriculums anymore. But later I found out that I was wrong.

The pastor asked me to produce a curriculum for a nine-month school, with classes meeting five days a week and three hours a day. By relying upon the ability God had placed inside me, I developed the curriculum for this school. I had doubled my ability! I was being more productive for the kingdom of God.

DOUBLING AGAIN AND AGAIN

Shortly afterward, I began to travel and teach God's Word. I thought that I would never have to develop another curriculum, but God had other thoughts in mind. Later that year, I was attending a church convention in Fort Worth, Texas. While sitting in a service the Lord spoke to my heart and let me know that I would be involved with starting training centers throughout the nation and around the world. At the same time, the Lord dealt with me about moving to Tulsa, Oklahoma.

When I finished the initial five-day-a week course for the training center in California, I did not realize the impact this would have upon my life and ministry. It was then that I left California and moved to Tulsa.

Once I had settled my family in Tulsa, I met with the pastors of a large fellowship there. One of these men mentioned that their Bible school was to open in Jamaica in September of that year. They had the facilities, the students, and the teacher. It was ready to start. All they needed was a curriculum, and I said, "I just happen to have one in my briefcase."

They told me what they needed and we produced a nine-month Bible course. It was a curriculum incorporating 162 lessons on faith, 162 lessons on spiritual emphasis subjects (e.g., The Blood Covenant, Gifts of the Spirit, Practical Ministries), and 324 lessons on expository and additional classes (e.g. New Testament Survey, Sermon Preparation, The Book of Revelation).

This curriculum became the World Outreach Bible Institute, now being used extensively around the world. At the request of many pastors in America, the curriculum has been modified of use in their churches.

This personal experience ties in directly with the object of Jesus' parable in *Matthew 25*--every man was given according to his own ability. God knew the ability I had, so He allowed me to produce according to that ability.

By being faithful to what God had for me to do, I constantly doubled my ability and my effectiveness. If I had trained and sent out ten ministers, I would have increased my effectiveness tenfold. The people I trained would affect others that I could never reach personally by going out and holding seminars. I have, in essence, duplicated myself in those who have been trained with the curriculum.

Numerically, we have seen outstanding results. In California the first graduating class to use the initial curriculum numbered 27 students. The second class graduated 200--all from the southern California area. The next group using an expanded curriculum included graduates from the schools in England, Guatemala, and Jamaica. We now have students enrolled in schools throughout the world. Can you see the parallel in this? By remaining faithful and diligent and doing what is at hand to the best of your ability, you will double your ability and effectiveness.

CHAPTER 5   Singleness of Heart

The senior pastor of our church in California was on the road quite a bit, but I was always in the office. A member of the congregation kept calling for counseling. Whenever she called, she would first ask for the senior pastor. Then she would ask for one of the other ministers.

Usually, neither of them was in, so she would say, "Well, who is there?" The receptionist would say, "Pastor Mike is here." So, she would talk to me. I gave her good counsel--whatever the Word said about her problem. Then we would pray.

I was doing the will of God from my heart and doing it with singleness of heart. She would say to me, "I tried to get the pastor, but he's not available! Then, I tried to get one of the other ministers, but he wasn't available either. So, because you're here, I'm stuck with you." But she began to change and grow. And it was a thrill for me to be able to watch her transformation and growth.

One day she called and asked for prayer as she had decided to sell her house. We prayed in agreement and the house sold quickly. The next Sunday morning she came with an envelope. As she walked up to me, she was all smiles. She said, "It's my joy and pleasure to do this, because no one else was ever around when I needed prayer. But you were always there. Here, I want you to have this."

I opened the envelope and inside was a check made out to me for $5,000! Oh, I tell you--that was enjoyable! (But this happened because I had been available whenever she had called, during the previous two years.) So, do the will of God from your heart, because God will cause you to be rewarded.

SELFLESS COMMITMENT

One word in the New Testament that deals with being a servant and giving service is *doulos*, which implies a totally selfless commitment to another. Vine says this word is used "frequently-- indicating subjection without the idea of bondage."

In other words, everything that the servant does is a total selfless commitment to another, to his master. Everything he does is designed to bring honor and glory to his master and not to himself. He's interested in doing whatever he can to benefit his master--not what will benefit himself.

Although a *doulos* is totally subjected to the master, there's no bondage involved at all. In our culture it's hard to conceive of that. Can you imagine being under the total control and influence of someone else without bondage? When Paul talks about being a servant of Jesus Christ, he uses the word *doulos*--yet there is no implication of bondage.

An equivalent Hebrew word was used in the Old Testament and translated "bond slave." In *Exodus 21:1-6* we read:

"Now these are the judgments which thou shall set before them. If thou buy a Hebrew servant, six years he shall serve: and in the seventh he shall go out free for nothing. If he came in by himself, he shall go out by himself: if he were married, then his wife shall go out with him. If his master has given him a wife and she has born him sons or daughters; the wife and her children shall be her master's and he shall go out by himself. And if the servant shall plainly say, I love my master, my wife, and my children; I will not go out free: Then his master shall bring him unto the judges; he shall also bring him to the door, or unto the door post; and his master shall bore his ear through with an awl; and he shall serve him forever." Exodus 21:1-6

In other words, they pierced the ear lobe as a sign of total servitude. The concept here is that if a love relationship developed and the servant did not want to go free, he was taken to the judges in the city where he made know his desire to become a bondservant to his master. A hole was then made in his ear as a legal sign. That hole would signify the fact that this person had ceased to exist as himself, and now was to be totally identified with his master.

He didn't just serve the man and work for wages, but became totally identified with and one with his master. No longer was he just a servant but a member of the household—part of the family. He would never leave, and his master became totally responsible for his every need. *Philippians 4:19* says: *"But my God shall supply all your need according to His riches in glory by Christ Jesus."*

A similar passage to the one in Exodus is found in *Deuteronomy 15:12-13: "And if thy brother, a Hebrew man, or a Hebrew woman, be sold unto thee and serve thee six years; then in the seventh year thou shall let him go free from thee."* Now notice this: *"And when thou send him out free from thee, thou shall not let him go away empty."*

After six years of service, if a servant wanted to go free, the master wasn't to send him away empty-handed. He wasn't to say, "You came here with nothing and you are leaving with nothing." Instead, he was to say, "You came here with nothing, and now I'm sending you out increased with goods. I'm giving you a part of everything you have helped me to gain."

Verse 15 of that chapter continues, *"And thou shall remember that thou were a bondman in the land of Egypt and the Lord thy God redeemed thee: therefore I command thee this thing today."*

In other words, God told the Israelites that when they set free a servant, it was to be as it was when God set them free from the land of Egypt.

He sent them out with silver, gold, jewels, cattle, and sheep. He increased them. So when a servant left, they were to make sure he went out well blessed.

"And it shall be, if he says unto thee, I will not go away from thee; because he loves thee and your house, because he is well with thee; Then thou shall take an awl and thrust it through his ear unto the door and he shall be thy servant forever. And also unto they maidservant thou shall do likewise" (Deuteronomy 15:16-17).

Picture this in your mind. You are ready to send your servant off well supplied. You are going to increase him in cattle, in grain, in wine, and in goods. He is going away with his pockets full and overflowing. But a love relationship has developed between you. He says, "All that increase is great, but I don't want to go. I want to serve you."

That must mean the master has taken good care of that individual. The master is saying, "Here, you can have all this." The individual is saying, "Hey, listen, its better off here than it is out there in the world."

If you have a company and you want to keep employees, make it so attractive for them and take such good care of them that, if somebody comes and offers them more money, they won't leave because money isn't the most important thing to them.

NOT ENOUGH SERVANTS

We have been talking about singleness of heart, about having a servant's attitude, and about the determination that you are going to serve--serving with singleness of heart. One of the problems within the Body of Christ today is that we don't have many servants.

Paul says in *Philippians 2:19-21: "But I trust in the Lord Jesus to send Timothy shortly unto you . . . For I have no man likeminded who will naturally care for your state. For all seek their own, not the things which are Jesus Christ's."*

Paul said the only person he could send them was Timothy, because he was the only one available who would be concerned about them and not about his pocketbook. Timothy had singleness of heart, and so did Paul. And both considered themselves servants. When you are a servant, God can use you because you will be faithful.

Paul says in *1 Corinthians 4:2* that faithfulness is required of a steward, a servant of God. There is no higher calling in life than to be a servant of God, and to be faithful or single-minded. But you cannot be this kind of servant until you are full of the life and nature of God--until you have the mind of Christ.

MADE FREE TO SERVE

Paul talks about another attribute of a servant of God in Romans chapter 1. He says we're to live a "separated life"; to be "separated unto the gospel of God." Now some people have a funny idea of what that means. Time and again I've heard people say something like, "I'm free. I don't have to go to church. I've got liberty. Jesus told me to stand fast in the liberty wherewith Christ made me free. I'm not going to be entangled in the yoke of bondage again. Nobody is going to put bondage on me."

When did going to church become bondage? Paul said: *"All things are lawful unto me, but all things are not expedient" (1 Corinthians 6:12)*. Also, when some people say they are "free", apparently they mean they are free to sin--to do things they don't need to be doing.

"I'm free; therefore I can go down to the bar and have a drink or two." The Bible also says: *"But now being made free from sin, and become servants to God, ye have your fruit unto holiness and the end everlasting life" (Romans 6:22)*.

You have been made free, not to sin or to do your own thing, but to become a servant of God. You aren't free to do anything that you might want to do. Before you were recreated, you didn't have a choice. Your nature caused you to sin. You were in bondage to Satan. Now you are free not to sin. That's what true freedom is. Being a servant is a thing of freedom.

Jesus had the attitude of a servant. *Matthew 10:24-25* says: *"The disciple is not above his master, nor the servant above his lord. It is enough for the disciple that he is as his master and the servant as his lord."*

People get the inflated idea that because they hold a certain office in the Body, or operate in certain ministries of the gifts of the Spirit, that they're something great. Not so. Jesus said, "The disciple is as his master, the servant as his lord."

CHAPTER 6   Function of a Servant

I have been teaching for many years about the ministry gifts and about the need to honor those gifts. It is true that we do need to honor the ministry gifts because they are gifts to the church from God. They are given to minister to us and cause us to be effective.

When we receive ministry gifts, we are saying to God, "Thank You for the opportunity you have given me to administer this gift to the church." But you have to receive it, or it is not useful to you--and you cannot make it useful to the church.

Some individuals have a mistaken attitude about the gifts of the Spirit. Instead of understanding that the gift is to the church and they are to administer it, they get the idea that they are the gift!

They act like this: "I'm a gift. You'd better treat me right because I'm a gift to you." Or like this: "Don't come near me. Don't touch me--I'm a gift. I don't want to talk to people--I'm going to go pray. I'm going to be God's person of faith and power."

Have you seen that kind of person? Instead of being good stewards and concerned about God requiring an account of the administration of the gift He gave them for the church, these people are all flash and no bang. They think they are faith and power when they are really just paste and flour.

While ministering in a powerful three-day meeting for a friend of mine in the state of Washington, he kept shaking his head. Finally, I asked him, "Brother, what's wrong?" He said, "You're not like any other traveling minister that I know." I said, "What do you mean?"

He explained that all the traveling ministers whom he had come in contact with would wait in the wings until the worship service was over. When it came time to introduce them, then they would appear. They would minister the Word, minister to the people, and then quickly go out the back door. They were untouchable.

But I have a pastor's heart, and I love the people. I don't want to run out the back door. I want to fellowship with people. Now, understand, some individuals have to leave quickly--and I've had *to modify my normal behavior overseas, where* you have crowds of 10,000 to 15,000 people in a meeting.

In very large meetings, the evangelist can't stick around to fellowship. If he fellowshipped with one, he would leave out the multitude. The only way to treat everybody fairly is not to give anyone special attention. But in small to medium-sized meetings, staying away from the people can be a sign of wrong attitude.

Paul said, "What I am is a servant. I am not anything else. I'm a servant of Jesus Christ." When I realize that I'm a servant, it takes away all the inner turmoil and strife--all the competition. Because I'm a servant, I'm responsible only for carrying out the instructions of my Master.

Secondly, in *Romans 1:1* Paul said he was called to be an apostle. *"To be"* is in italics in the Bible, so it's not in the original Greek, but added by the translator for our understanding. The passage could be read this way: "Paul, a servant of Jesus Christ, called an apostle." Paul was saying, "What I am is a servant. How I function is an apostle."

In *Ephesians 4:11* it says that Jesus gave gifts unto men: *"And he gave some, apostles; and some, prophets; and some, evangelists; and some, pastors and teachers."* We call these the five-fold ministry gifts.

Then in *1 Corinthians 12:28* Paul says: *"And God hath set some in the church, first apostles, secondarily prophets, thirdly teachers, after that miracles, then gifts of healings, helps, governments, diversities of tongues."*

We used to try to make those two verses mesh in this way: In *1 Corinthians 12:28* Paul says, "apostles, prophets, and teachers," so those three are taken care of. But it also says "miracles and gifts of healings," so that has to be the evangelist. Exciting things happen for the evangelist. Then we have "helps, governments, and diversities of tongues," so that must be the ministry of the pastor.

In recent years, however, we've learned that there's a ministry of helps, a supernatural ministry where an individual is called by God. There are people who get involved in helping, but who aren't called specifically into such a ministry. But those who are placed by God into this kind of ministry are just as important as the apostle, prophet, evangelist, pastor, or teacher.

FUNCTIONS ARE NOT TITLES

Such as the ministry of government, administration or "ruling," and the ministry of tongues, these verses about ministries left people with many questions. I used to ponder over *Ephesians 4:11* and *1 Corinthians 12:28*, but they just wouldn't fit together. Something was wrong with my understanding.

I was in a service on a Sunday morning when the pastor made this statement in his preaching, "You know, I've been studying, praying, and asking God about Ephesians 4, and the Lord said to me: "I never meant those as positions or titles. I meant those as job descriptions.""

People have taken their job description and elevated it and said that's what they are. No, those listings are just ***descriptions*** of their jobs. Those ministries are functional titles--names designating where an individual functions--not what an individual is.

During this century, the Holy Spirit has emphasized certain ministries. He has emphasized the apostle's ministry and the prophet's ministry. It seemed everyone wanted to be an apostle or prophet. Nobody wanted to be a pastor.

Then there came an emphasis on the pastor's ministry. Now we have a whole generation of people walking around saying, "I'm an apostle, I'm a prophet, I am a pastor, I'm an evangelist, I am a teacher, I am this, I am that . . ." The big "I" --the big "me." And where is Jesus in all this?

Paul was saying in *Romans 1:1* that he was a servant who functioned as an apostle, "a sent one." When I become a love slave of Jesus Christ--when everything I do is viewed in relationship to causing His will to be done--then my function does not matter because my function is not what I am--it's what I do.

When people get upset because they are working as a janitor, it's because they believe a janitor is what they are. That's not what they are-- that is just where they are function. Your function is not you. You are a servant of Jesus Christ. What does it matter how you function if you're doing it with singleness of motive--doing it as unto the Lord, doing the will of God from singleness of heart?

As a servant of Jesus, your function is determined by Him, the Master, and not by yourself. The servant is viewed in relationship to his Master. You're not viewed by God in relationship to your work, but in relationship to Jesus.

It doesn't matter how you function: apostle, prophet, evangelist, pastor, teacher, janitor, counselor, usher, host, hostess, or anywhere else; it helps. It doesn't matter--because what you are is a servant.

When God dealt with me about the idea of the attitude of a servant, I got out my Strong's Concordance and wrote down every Scripture reference that had the word *servant* in it. Then I went through my Bible and put an asterisk by the references on my list that applied and crossing out the ones that didn't apply.

When I came to *Romans 1:1*, I read it and started to cross it out. But the Spirit of the Lord said, "No, go back and read it again." I said, "Well, it doesn't say anything." The Lord said, "Go back and read it again. *Romans 1:1* is a salutation. It's the very beginning of the long letter we know as a "book." And I used to read the salutations the same way I read the genealogy of Christ in Matthew and Luke . . . "begat, begat, begat, begat, begat, begat." I read through it quickly.

I had done this with *Romans 1:1*; *"Paul, a servant of Jesus Christ, called to be an apostle, separated unto the gospel of God.*" I would try to go on. But God just kept bringing me back to it. I decided to meditate on it, because apparently there was something I wasn't seeing.

When my eyes finally were opened to what the verse really was saying, it was 2:00 a.m. I had to keep quiet because I was ministering in New Jersey and staying in the pastor's home--but it sure was hard to be silent!

Here, in one verse of Scripture--a salutation, at that--you see the whole heart and attitude of the Apostle Paul. In that one verse, he tells us everything we need to know to be successful. He tells us who he is, how he functions, and how he lives. He was a servant functioning as an apostle and living separated from the world.

I came out of the Hippie culture of the 1960's. In that era, we were trying to "tune in, turn on, and drop out." We were experimenting with mind-altering drugs in an attempt to find out who we were. It was a search for identity. But you can't find out who you are until you are born again. Then only, you find out who you are in Christ. Once you find that out, then you can begin to do something for God.

Even in the Body of Christ a lot of people are trying to find out who they are: "Who am I? What am I? Who am I, God?" Paul said, "I am a *doulos*, a bond servant." In other words, "I am Paul, the *doulos*, the servant of Jesus Christ. I am Christ's servant, God's servant. I am a love servant. When Christ set me free on the road to Damascus, I chose to be his servant for life. Now I don't live--He lives in me. What I am is a servant."

ELEMENTS OF SERVANTHOOD

Some people change their attitudes toward me when they find that I am the author of *Supportive Ministries*. Sometimes they change their attitude when they find I am on the staff of a large ministry. And that isn't the right attitude.

I am not viewed in relationship to my work. I am viewed in the relationship to my Master. I am a servant of Jesus Christ. When you realize that you are a servant and that who you are, then your function doesn't matter because the function is determined by the Master. You are not viewed in relationship to your function; you are viewed in relationship to your Master.

"Oh, you work for ***that*** ministry?"

"Yes."

Then someone thinks, "I'd better treat him well, because he works for that large church." That's the wrong attitude. You have to treat me well because I'm a servant of Jesus Christ.

I was teaching at a church, and they put me in an economy motel. I went over to the church and talked with the associate pastor. I said, "Brother,

I'm not trying to cause any problem, but I've been on the road two weeks. I appreciate the room you gave me, but it's quite small. There is another motel right down the road that has larger rooms and better facilities. I'd rather stay there. I will pay the difference. I'm not concerned about that. I just would like a comfortable place to stay." The associate pastor said, "Not a problem."

They put me up at the other motel and took care of the bill. I was talking with the associate pastor later that week, and he asked me several things about the traveling ministry. Accommodations were one of the things he wanted to know about. I said, "Just use this rule of thumb: How would you like to be treated?"

A traveling minister spends his time on the road. He's in one motel room after another, after another. Where would you want to stay if you were constantly away from home and living in hotels? Would you like to stay in a small room where everything is cramped, or would you like to have someplace where you could walk and pray and have a little bit of space? He said, "Ah ha! Now I understand."

So, I believe it will be better in the future for all the others who go to minister in that church. I could have had the attitude, "Well, how dare you put me in such a small room? This is beneath my dignity." But I didn't approach it that way at all. I approached it with an attitude of consideration for my hosts--by offering to pay the difference out of my own pocket.

FUNCTIONS CHOSEN BY GOD

We're servants of God and viewed in relationship to that. What we do and how we function doesn't matter. When we're viewed in relationship to God, He will cause us to function in whatever capacity He needs at that given point in time.

You might function primarily as a teacher, which is my primary function in the Body. But I'm not a teacher--I'm a servant. If I get my mind set that, "I'm a teacher, I'm a teacher, I'm a teacher", and I believe that's all I am, I have just cut myself off from God using me in any other way but as a teacher. But when I say, "I'm a servant," then my function becomes determined by the Master and not by me. God can have me function as a teacher, or as an apostle, or as a prophet--for I am just a servant.

At one church in New Jersey, the Lord has used me several times as a prophet. Did I try to be? No. Did they pray that I would be a prophet to the church? No. I've been there several times and each time the Lord has used me in a prophetic anointing to set expose some things and set them in order.

It began with a three--day seminar on the Ministry of Helps. I didn't know they were having problems. I made a simple statement and I said it just like this, "If you don't agree with the vision of the pastor, there's the back door. Don't let it hit you on the way out." But then I explained, "Now, what I mean to say is that if you can't agree with the pastor's vision, you need to find some place where you can agree. You need to find another place to hook up. So, there's the door. Don't let it hit you. Don't make problems. Just resign."

That week, eleven of his workers resigned. The pastor called me the next week and said, "Well, brother, your seminar was a turning point." I said, "Oh, really?" At first I thought, "Great!" But then he said, "Yes, I had eleven workers leave." I sighed, "Oh." He explained, "But the next Sunday morning, God gave us fifty new people." He was excited, and the church grew.

The next time when I was in that town, the same congregation asked me to come and minister. They purposely would not tell me what was going on. They were praying that God would use me in that prophetic vain to expose and correct the problems that they were experiencing in the church.

I prayed, "Oh, dear God, I don't think I want to preach tonight." When they asked what I would be preaching on, I told them I would preach on the mercy of God. They questioned, "Are you sure?" In spite of their question, I preached on mercy and it handled the problems. I got off on what I thought was a side trail, and God moved.

A group of people rose up after that and were angry. They went to the pastor and said, "How dare you tell him everything that's going on in this church? You told him what was going on and you told him what to say!"

The Holy Spirit exposed everything that was going on through my sermon. These people thought the pastor had set them up to be preached at, and as a result the four families that had been causing problems left the church; but the next week 100 new people came to the church.

The third time I was there, they said, "Well, praise God! Brother Mike is coming. Bring your asbestos suits. We love to be corrected and rebuked by the Word." When the leaders told me how they'd promoted my visit, I thought nobody would show up. But the place was full and the same thing happened again. Problem people left and God added 50 new people.

To that church, I functioned as a prophet. The Spirit of God would just show me things, and I would correct the problems. I didn't go in there trying to be a prophet. I would pray, "God, give me a nice, simple, sweet message. I want to be loved. I don't want to be known as the guy that brings the fire."

I ministered at that church three times and as a result the church increased by 200 people. The increase didn't come by me being there. The increase came after I functioned there as a prophet and the dead weight left. To that church I was a prophet. Am I a prophet? No. I'm a servant of Jesus Christ. As a servant, I'll function any way the Master needs me to function.

The late Rev. Dick Mills, who functioned primarily as a prophet, asked me to share with his staff about the Attitude of a Servant. When I shared the concepts that are in this book and we talked afterwards, he said, "You've answered a question for me."

He explained, "I usually stay in the ministry of a prophet, but I have gone into some churches where all I could do was teach. I would go to the next place and have apostolic power. I would then go someplace else, and all I could do was preach an evangelistic message. I would go to another meeting, and all I could do was pastor the people.

What you shared today enlarged my perspective. I'm a servant and--as a servant--my function doesn't matter. God can use me in whatever function is necessary at the time." But you can't be like that until you are a servant. All those people who are running around saying they're this, that, and the other thing are sadly mistaken. They are servants.

People need to understand and recognize where they primarily function, but the easiest way of doing it is by realizing their status as servants. When they begin to operate as servants, they begin to serve God in the way which He desires. Their function will not remain the same--it will constantly change.

PERSONAL EXAMPLES

I had been on the staff of a Full Gospel church for four and a half years, working my way up from janitor to associate pastor. Then I spent four and a half months with a Jewish outreach ministry. In this latter ministry, they did not believe certain things that I believed. It got to the point where the differences were quite noticeable and could have caused a split in the church.

I was teaching the truths of the integrity of God's Word, restored by the Holy Spirit to the Body of Christ during the last 50 years, and they were teaching against it. I would say one thing and the senior pastor would say the opposite. People would come to me saying, "What's going on? We can see in the Word that what you are saying is true, but he is against it. What are we going to do?"

I started praying about the situation. Then I went to the pastor, resigned, and left town. Six months later, they asked me to come back and preach. I preached, and the Holy Spirit turned that place right-side-up. As a result, some four months later the pastor brought in an associate who understood the things of the Spirit. But he wasn't ready to receive the truth of the Word while I was there. So, rather than cause division or strife, I left.

Soon after, I was asked to be the assistant pastor of a growing church in Palos Verdes, California. I preached all the time--almost every Sunday evening and Wednesday evening. I was thanking God that He called me to preach and teach. That's all I wanted to do.

Then in August of that year, after I'd been with that church for six months, God began to deal with me about administration. But I didn't want to hear it. In fact, I remember the Wednesday night when He first spoke to me about adding administration to my function.

The Lord said, "I want you to tell the senior pastor that I am going to send him an administrator whose salary is already paid." I remember arguing with the Lord over that. I thought, "That's ridiculous." But I went to him and I said, "The Lord just told me to tell you this. I might sound ridiculous and I don't know how He's going to do it, but He said that He's going to send you an administrator whose salary is already paid."

Little did I know that it was me! A few weeks later, on a Sunday morning, the senior pastor asked if my wife, Martha, was in the service. When I told him she was, she said, "I've got to minister to you. I have a word from the Lord for you."

I thought, "Glory to God, it's time for my radio ministry." That was a big thing back then. Everybody was going on the radio. I thought I would have a radio ministry and maybe a newsletter. So he called my wife and I up in front of the entire congregation and said, "Mike, are you willing to administrate?" And I immediately said "Yes." I'd made an adjustment in my attitude. It took me about three seconds to make that adjustment on the inside. Then I said, "Yes."

And the Spirit of the Lord ministered through him and said, "If you will be faithful for two years, I will release you to that which you desire to do." At that time, I desired to travel and teach. But I stayed with him, pastored, administrated the church, and ran the Bible training center. We gained national prominence. And it was interesting that in the month of August, exactly two years later, to the day, I left that ministry and began a traveling teaching ministry.

I traveled across the nation for a year with tremendous results: miracles, signs and wonders. Then I became a member of the pastoral staff of Faith Christian Fellowship in Tulsa, and Dean of the School of Helps. I had not even gotten to preach in the church before I became a staff member. Then they let me preach once in the church when everybody was out of town. Should I cry and complain? No. God told me to go serve the pastor, so I went to serve the pastor.

CALLED TO PASTOR

One day the Spirit of the Lord spoke to me and said, "You're going to be one of the pastors." When He told me that, I said, "Sure, I'm willing." But I didn't run to the pastor and tell him that I was going to be one of his pastors. No way; I waited on God to bring it to pass.

I put that prophetic word on the shelf and said, "OK, God, I know your voice and I believe this is you. Now you're going to have to tell the pastor." One of the biggest thrills I've ever had came while I was sitting at breakfast with the pastor one morning. He said, "Mike, have you ever considered Pastoring?" I knew already where he was going with that question, but I said, "If you mean going out and Pastoring my own church, no. That's not what God has in mind for me."

He said, "No, I didn't mean that. Mike, I need you to pastor our South Worship Hall. Would you rather do that, or continue doing what you are called and anointed to do: set up Bible schools across the nation and around the world? Which would you rather do?"

The pastor continued, "I know this is going to be a hard decision for you to make. Go ahead and pray about it. I answered, "I don't need to pray about it, Pastor." He looked surprised and replied, "you don't?" In response, I said, "No; God called me to serve you. What do you need me to do?" He then said; "Pastor the church." And my reply to him was,"Then that is what I will do."

I then informed him of what the Lord had spoken to me about being one of the pastors. He started telling me all the reasons why I should stay with the Bible schools--he wanted me to be sure in my own mind and spirit about the change of functions. I interjected. "Wait a minute, Pastor; I'm smart enough to realize that if God told me to serve you, and I serve you in whatever capacity is necessary, it will work out for the best. Even if I can't devote time to the schools now, they will be farther down the road when I finish doing what you need me to do, than if I were to act in disobedience and work on them that whole time."

That statement is truth, because even without spending a lot of time with Bible school curriculums, great strides have been made. We have obtained a relationship with a University in Hawaii which offers long distance learning programs for completing degree work. They have agreed to accept out courses as part of the credit necessary for individuals to obtain a degree in Biblical Studies with them. God orchestrated it and I did not have to peruse it; it pursued me.

WE HAVE GONE INTERNATIONAL!

The curriculum has also been translated into Finnish, Norwegian, Spanish, French, Russian, Polish, and Portuguese. The material is being used in the Philippines, Norway, Portugal, Kenya, England, Mexico, Ecuador, Lithuania, Poland, USA, Guatemala, Honduras, Belize, the Caribbean, and it continues to grow and expand to this day.

Now you see, God called me to start training centers. But I'm a servant. And by serving my pastor and doing what he needs to have done, more doors opened up for the Bible school curriculum than you can imagine. And I haven't had to pursue one of them! They came to me.

The truth of this principle has allowed the schools to expand at a rapid rate. The Lord directed my family and me to move to New Jersey. We obeyed the Lord, and He began to open doors I had previously dreamed of but did not see how they could ever become a reality.

The pastor of a church, Faith Fellowship Ministries, welcomed us with open arms. He encouraged me concerning the Bible schools and made all his television equipment available. This opened a whole new vista and increased the accessibility of the curriculum. We now have our material available in a distance learning format which enables churches to open a Bible school while they are developing a teaching staff. The curriculum available also provides the avenue to have a correspondence school.

It has taken many years to reach the point where I am now. I consider all those years as preparation for what I'm currently doing. If I had not been faithful to do what was at hand to do, I would still be back at square one.

PAUL'S PATHWAY INTO HIS MINISTRY

In *Acts 9* Paul was called as an apostle. In *Acts 13*, he was separated. That wasn't long--just 15 years. First he was called, and then 15 years later he was separated to the office or the ministry that he had been called into.

In fact, after he was called of God, the first thing he did was witness. Later he served as a teacher. Then he functioned as a prophet. After that, God thrust him back into what he had been called to do 15 years before.

But because he was a servant, Paul said, *"And I thank Christ Jesus our Lord, who hath enabled me, for that He counted me faithful, putting me into the ministry"* (*1 Timothy 1:12*). So, you see, when you count yourself as a servant--when you understand that a servant is who you are--then God can use you.

CHAPTER 7   The Paradox of Greatness

The Christian life is full of what seems to be paradoxes or contradictions, if judged by the standard of the world's system. The world says, "Take, or you won't get." The Word says, *"Give and it shall be given unto you" (Luke 6:38)*. It doesn't say, "Hold back for yourself." Jesus said that, unless you die, you cannot find life.

In *Romans 8:14-17* God says that we're no longer servants but children of God. The wording here show that we are, now that we are full grown, mature children. Our adoption is with full rights and privileges. As such we are free to become servants.

Jesus explains the paradox of greatness in *Mark 9:30-34:*

"And they departed thence and passed through Galilee; and he would not that any man should know it; For he taught his disciples and said unto them, The Son of man is delivered into the hands of men and they shall kill him and after that he is killed, he shall rise the third day. But they understood not that saying and were afraid to ask him. And he came to Capernaum: and being in the house he asked them, what was it that ye disputed among yourselves by the way? But they held their peace: for by the way they had disputed among themselves, who should be the greatest."

In the Church today, there seems to be quite a few individuals who are jealous and desirous of positions and speak against anyone who may be honored. They dispute among themselves who should be greatest, but never about serving. It seems that they are more concerned about being served than in serving.

"And He sat down and called the twelve and saith unto them, if any man desire to be first, the same shall be last of all and the servant of all" (Mark 9:35).

If you desire to be great, you must be the servant of all. Jesus' idea of greatness is service. Our idea of greatness is notoriety. The two ideas can go together, because if you are the servant of all, God will promote you to be known by all. But you will be known because of your service--not because of who you are. Most of the leaders in the Church today, both men and women are known because of their service to the Body of Christ.

SERVE FAITHFULLY

One message that has not been popular is that of service, but that is changing and now it's becoming more widely accepted. The truth of this message has not changed, and people are finally awaking to the fact that we are called to serve and not be served. If you focus on serving, then it will not matter to you if you are first or not. It is not about you, but about Him and ministering to others.

When you get to the point where all you care about is serving Jesus--doing what would please Him and benefit His kingdom--then promotion will began to come. It will not be a big deal. You could care less...you are serving the Lord.

DISCIPLES SEEKING GREATNESS

In the tenth chapter of Mark, the discussion was taken up again.

"And James and John, the sons of Zebedee, came unto Him, saying, Master, we would that thou should do for us whatsoever we shall desire. And He said unto them, what would ye that I should do for you? They said unto Him, grant unto us that we may sit, one on the right hand and the other on thy left hand, in thy glory" (Mark 10:35-37).

In essence, they were saying, "We don't want much; we just want to sit on your right hand and on your left hand in glory. We want the two positions of honor and esteem for eternity. Not much, you know!"

"But Jesus said unto them, you know not what ye ask: can ye drink of the cup that I drink of and be baptized with the baptism that I am baptized with? And they said unto Him, we can. And Jesus said unto them, Ye shall indeed drink of the cup

that I drink of; and with the baptism that I am baptized withal shall ye be baptized. But to sit on my right hand and on my left hand is not mine to give; but it shall be given to them for whom it is prepared. And when the ten heard it, they began to be much displeased with James and John" (Mark 10:38-41).

Now isn't that just like the multitude? You know why the other disciples got angry with James and John? They were thinking, "How dare they ask for position of authority--for the position of exaltation?" They thought James and John were going to get a place of honor and they weren't. They probably were angry because they didn't think to ask Jesus for it first.

STRIFE IN THE CAMP REVISITED

Remember when Jesus was transfigured? Peter, James, and John were on the mountaintop with Him and saw Him transfigured. When they came down from the Mount of Transfiguration, the disciples had been trying to cast the devil out of a young boy and could not. In *Matthew 17:21*, most of our translations say, *"Howbeit this kind goes not out but by prayer and fasting"* (c.f. *Mark 9:29*). Apparently that verse isn't the original, but was added later. The reason they could not cast out the demon. They had gone from faith to unbelief. I believe that strife and jealousy are what brought them to that point. It will get you working in the flesh and not in the Spirit.

They may have been saying, "Peter, James, and John, again. All the time it is just Peter, James, and John--it is not fair. When Jairus' daughter was raised from the dead, Peter, James, and John got to be there and we didn't. Man, did you see them on the mountain with thunder and lightning? God appeared just as He did with Moses. All that glory, and Peter, James, and John got to be there. And we've been stuck down here, trying to get a dumb devil out of this kid!"

"But Jesus called them to Him and saith unto them, "You know that they which are accounted to rule over the Gentiles exercise lordship over them; and their great ones exercise authority upon them" (Mark 10:42).

He was saying, in essence, "Listen, this is how the world does it. They rule and reign. They exercise the authority with ego and with pride. And if they have a position, they let everybody know about it."

"But so shall it not be among you: but whosoever will be great among you, shall be your minister: And whosoever of you will be the chiefest, shall be servant of all. For even the Son of man came not to be ministered unto, but to minister and to give His life a ransom for man" (Mark 10:43-45).

A SERVANT'S ATTITUDE

This last verse summarizes everything that Jesus did, and shows His attitude; *"The Attitude of a Servant."* He was essentially telling them, "I did not come to be ministered to. If I had wanted to be ministered to, I would have stayed in glory. I had all the angels ministering to me. I didn't come to be ministered to--I came to minister. I didn't come to get. I came to give."

There are a lot of people in the ministry who are trying to be ministered to and trying to get. People have found out that if they give, it's given to them. They give so they can get. But that is the wrong attitude.

The same idea is brought out in *Mathew 23:11:* *"But he that is greatest among you shall be your servant."* Jesus was saying, "You want to be great? You want to be the greatest one? I will show you how to be the greatest. Be the servant of everyone. The greatest among you shall be your servant."

"And whosoever shall exalt himself shall be abased; and he that shall humble himself shall be exalted" (Matthew 23:12).

As amazing as it sounds, I've been in places where ministers argued as to which gift was greatest, and who had the authority in that place according to the gift being manifested. They were ready to hurl lightning bolts at each other. "The prophet is greatest!" "No, the apostle is!"

WHO HAS THE HIGHEST AUTHORITY?

In the local church, nobody has greater authority than the pastor. The only churches Paul ever exercised authority over were those he started, and then only until God raised up a pastor for that congregation.

There is a ministry that helped start several churches in southern California. Their Superintendent of Churches who was their "prophet," began going around to the local groups saying, "You are credentialed with us, and I'm here to preach in your church." Most of the pastors he had used this on were foolish enough to let him preach. But one pastor stood up to him and said, "Well, that's news to me. I have a message from God to deliver today."

The Superintendent said, "But you don't understand, you are ordained with us. I'm a prophet, and I'm here to preach in your church." Standing firm, the pastor said, "I don't care. I'm the pastor, and you're not preaching in my church this morning. If you want to preach, give me a call and we will discuss a date. We will be more than happy to have you speak sometime, but you are not preaching in my church this morning."

The Superintendent persisted, "You don't understand. You're credentialed with us and I am a prophet. I'm here to preach." To which the pastor replied, "Oh, now I understand. I'll take care of it.

Just wait a second." He pulled out his wallet, took out his ministerial card issued by that church and ripped it into shreds. "There you are," he fumed. "Now, get out of my church." He later was ordained through another organization which had a greater influence and positive reputation in the church world. By standing strong, this pastor was emphasizing that apart from Jesus, the highest authority in the church is the pastor.

GOD'S SPIRIT GIVES DIRECTION

There is no higher authority than the pastor within the local church. The apostle will go from a church, and God will set prophets within a church. But a prophet doesn't give direction. The Spirit of God gives direction. The Bible doesn't say, "Those that are led by the prophets are the sons of God." It says that if you are led by the Spirit, you're a son of God (*Romans 8:14*).

When we get to heaven and the rewards are passed out, one individual may say, "Well, Jesus, I'm an apostle." And Jesus will give that person a little reward. Another individual may say, "I'm a prophet." Jesus will give him a little reward.

Then a third will come who will say, "Jesus, I'm a servant." When He hears that, Jesus will turn and say, "Sound the trumpet! Everybody line the streets. We are going to have a parade. We've got a servant! Finally, we have someone who deserves a triumphant entry; who truly represents the King and His kingdom."

2 Peter 1:11 says there will be an *abundant entrance* opened to you in the kingdom of heaven. Do you know what that means? The gates will be flung wide, and there will be a ticker-tape parade. That's how I want to go in. Jesus said the greatest is going to be the servant of all.

CHAPTER 8   The Example of Jesus

A SERVANT'S ATTITUDE REVEALED

Jesus gave us an example of a servant's attitude, as recorded in *John 13:2-4:*

"And supper being ended, the devil having now put into the heart of Judas Iscariot, Simon's son, to betray Him; Jesus knowing that the Father had given all things into His hands and that He was come from God and went to God; He rises from supper and laid aside his garments; and took a towel and girded himself."

History tells us that the towel He picked up was called the "servant's towel." It represented the office of the lowest slave. The slave that washed and wiped people's feet was the lowest of the low. That wasn't the bottom of the barrel--it was underneath the barrel. Jesus, King of kings and Lord of lords, took that servant's towel and began to wash the disciples' feet. He was the King of glory, yet He came to earth and made Himself the lowest of the low.

"After that he poured water into a basin and began to wash the disciples' feet and to wipe them with the towel wherewith he was girded: (John 13:5).

I can just see Peter watching and thinking, "He shouldn't be doing that. He is the Messiah. He can't be doing that."

"Then cometh He to Simon Peter: and Peter saith unto Him, Lord, dost thou wash my feet? Jesus answered and said unto him, what I do you know not now; but thou shall know hereafter. Peter saith unto Him, Thou shall never wash my feet. Jesus answered him; if I wash thee not, though hast no part of me. Simon Peter said unto Him; Lord, Not my feet only, but also my hands and my head: (John 13:6-9).

I like Peter's honesty along with his impetuousness. First he tells Jesus, "You will never wash my feet." He's saying, "You are too good to do that, Lord." But once Jesus tells Peter he will not have any part in the Kingdom unless he allows Him to wash his feet, Peter's attitude changes drastically. He then not only wants his feet washed, but his head and hands as well! In other words, Peter is saying, "I don't want just a part--I want all." That's a true servant's heart. He wants to serve his master completely.

I love Jesus' response to Peter:

"Jesus said to him, He that is washed needs not save to wash his feet, but is clean every whit: and ye are clean, but not all. For he knew who should betray Him; therefore, said he, you are not all clean" (John 13:10-11).

Jesus used even His last supper with the disciples as an opportunity to teach. He said, in essence, "Listen, you are clean through the Word that I have given to you. When you're born again and filled with the Spirit, you are clean. You are not of this world, but you are in this world. When you get your feet a little bit dirty from walking in the world, the Word I have given you washes them off."

'If we confess our sins, he is faithful and just to forgive our sins and to cleanse us from all unrighteousness" (1 John 1:9).

"So after he had washed their feet and had taken his garments and was set down again, he said unto them know you what I have done to you?" (John 13:12).

I am sure they were saying, "Yeah, yeah, you washed our feet." But He said:

"Ye call me Master and Lord: and ye say well; for so I am. If I then, your Lord and Master, have washed your feet; ye also ought to wash one another's feet. For I have given you an example, that ye should do as I have done to you" (John 13:13-15).

People have taken this portion of Scripture and used it to implement and institute foot washing services as a doctrine. But He was not talking about having a foot-washing service. What He was saying in essence was:

"Listen, I have given you an example. If I, being your Master and Lord, can serve you, then you can surely serve one another. Listen, if I, your Master and Lord, have washed your feet, so you ought to do be able to do it for one another. I have given you an example. If I can humble myself and do this, then you can humble yourselves to serve one another. If you want to be great, then be the servant of all."

"Verily, verily, I say unto you, the servant is not greater than his lord; neither is he that is sent greater than he that sent him. If ye know these things, happy are ye if ye do them" (John 13:16-17).

He said, "It is not enough to just know these things, you have got to do them." In other words, your motive in doing things for the Lord is to serve, not to be exalted. When Jesus fed the multitude, He did it to serve them, to meet their needs, not to be exalted. And we should all *go, and do likewise.* To be happy, you have to do the works.

UNHAPPY PEOPLE

There are some who have not embraced this truth. They constantly want to be served rather than to serve. They have forgotten where they have come from and their initial first love. It was to do whatever the Lord had for them, and not based upon what they would receive in return. We must serve out of love for God and the people.

When we forget this, we become unhappy and complain.

The people are miserable because they feel they are not doing enough, and the pastors are miserable and have lost the joy of serving. Everyone is miserable, and they think it will be worth it all when they get to heaven. Thanks be to God, it can be worth it all down here!

It revolves around your attitude. Jesus tried to impress the disciples to maintain the attitude of a servant through His example and teaching. He wanted them and he wants us to develop an *attitude of service.* This will make us look more like Him.

FINDING WHERE YOU FIT

When you are wondering where you fit in the plan and scope of things, just keep these simple points in mind:

Step 1: Realize you are called of God. Whether you are a prayer intercessor or one who financially supports the ministry, you are called!

Step 2: Make a quality decision to fulfill the position God has called you to. Remember: let God promote you; don't promote yourself.

Step 3: Whatever your hand finds to do, do it. Ecclesiastes 9:10 says; *"Whatsoever, your hand finds to do, do it with all your might."* Not halfheartedly – with all your might! *Matthew 20:16* says, *Many are called, but few are chosen.* It is not enough to be called. Once you are called, you have to get involved and start doing. Whatever your hand finds to do, do it. Become involved; then you will be chosen. I know of many people who were called, but they were not faithful long enough to be chosen. When this happens, people always blame God when it was their own fault.

Step 4: Do not attempt to walk in another man's calling. If you try it, it will only lead to frustration. Attempting to walk in another man's calling will only take you out of the will of God, making you an open target for Satan, and he will snuff you out as quickly as he can! The Lord will attempt to warn you, but if you don't stop, there is nothing God can do.

You must allow God to use you as He wants, with your own personality traits. It is God that calls you; you do not call yourself. Let me share from personal experience as an example.

When I was first born again and filled with the Spirit, I remember how excited I was. I wanted to get involved in a church and do something for God. I began working in a half-way house just because I loved God. I was making $25 a week and thought it was the "big time." I was in the ministry, and that was all that was important. After seven months, I had used up all the money in my savings account, but I couldn't have cared less. I was happy to be involved in the things of God. To me, it was the greatest honor in the world to work for God and actually get paid for it!

The pastor of the church I attended would walk to the pulpit on Sunday with his big, black notebook full of notes, open it, and begin to preach. So, the first opportunity I was given to preach in that church, I walked up with my two Bibles and a big, black notebook full of notes. I opened the notebook and began. The service was dry!

After that experience, I wondered if I was really called to preach. I decided, the next time I was given the opportunity to preach that I would just be myself and let God use me; just as I was. When that time came, I did just that. I used humor and allowed my personality to come through my preaching. I ministered the Word of God from my heart. Many in the congregation understood what I was preaching and had their needs met. I let God use me and my personality.

You will have success if you just be yourself. Don't try to copy someone else.

Another time, I tried to copy a pastor who was sixty years old and had been in the ministry for forty years. He would get up at 4:30 every morning to pray and read the Word. I decided to do the same thing so that I could be spiritual like he was. But I didn't realize that he was in bed before nine o'clock almost every evening, while I had the young people over to my house and didn't get to bed until about midnight. I would get up at 4:30 a.m., throw some cold water on my face, go to the front room, get down on my knees by a chair, and begin to pray. The next thing I knew, it was 8:00 and I was just waking up – again!

I became frustrated with myself and was certain that God would never use me. Then the Lord pointed out the fact that it was not getting up at 4:30 a.m. that caused success in that man of God, it was his diligence and consistency that brought the results. So I adjusted my prayer time to my schedule; the frustration left me and I began to have success. I was being myself, and God was using me. I found out then that I couldn't walk in someone else's calling; neither could they walk in mine.

You have to reach that place and realize: "I'm called of God, fulfilling what God has for me right now." Then you will relax in the things of God. You will not be pushing, trying to get there; you will see that you are there.

When you know you are called of God, you won't be affected by the things that happen around you. When someone else ministers, you won't be bothered in the least. You will rejoice in what the Lord is doing. You realize that people's needs are being met and that is what is important. You remain focused on what the Lord has called you to do, and the people he has sent for you to minister to.

CONCLUSION

In this book I have attempted to impart to you what I have learned over the past 43 years of ministry. It is my desire that you understand and embrace these truths and that you can glean from this material and not have to go through the same process that I went through.

It is important that we recognize that God has placed not only people to fill senior positions, but that He has also established supportive positions. These supportive roles are vital for the fulfillment of any dream or ministry to be successful.

We have seen that God places a premium on faithfulness. It is major requirement of all His stewards. Without our faithfulness, we become clouds tossed back and forth with every wind that blows our way. God rewards faithfulness with an abundance of internal peace and well being.

The attitude that motivates your behavior will determine the outcome of your situation, and -- ultimately-of your life. Your attitude controls how others react to you. Your attitude controls how you react to others and to the Lord. You have been saved for a purpose and that is to serve God.

When you allow this mindset, (the mind of Christ), to take root in you, and consider yourself a bond servant to Him, you will find yourself totally identified with Him. Your desire will be to serve, and your life will be one of meeting the needs of others and lifting up Jesus.

The world seeks to exalt itself; this is the nature of Satan. The Christian seeks to exalt Jesus, and focuses all attention toward Him. When you do this and maintain the proper attitude, the particular function in which God has sent you to perform becomes your "job" in the Kingdom. Your function is your responsibility, for which you will have to give an account. It won't become a means for self-exaltation.

REMEMBER

YOU ARE NOT YOUR FUNCTION.
YOU ARE A SERVANT (DOULOS).

It is my prayer that you embrace the truth presented here, and you develop the same attitude that Jesus had--the *Attitude of a Servant.*

A SPECIAL THANK YOU

While preparing to write this book, my mind went back to the various individuals who have had dramatic effects upon my life. All of them had one thing in common: The Attitude of a Servant. The whole desire of these people was to obey God's call upon their lives and to help people.

I have been blessed to have several individuals who have had a major impact upon my life and ministry. My first Pastor, the late Herb Ezell, taught me discipline and commitment to God and to His Church and helped cultivate that heart into me: Buddy and Pat Harrison saw the gifting and made room for me to grow and utilize my gifts in helping them accomplish their God given assignment.

Pastor David and Diane Demola provided an avenue that allowed me to employ my talents and giftings to help them fulfill their mandate from God. They have been a consistent example of dedication and selfless commitment to the Lord and His work.

Pastor Joseph and Wendy Prince have been good friends and a constant encouragement to us, both in fellowship and support. Their entire staff manifests the Grace of God, and operates with a spirit of excellence; they depict a Servant's heart. Martha and I draw strength from them and the confidence they have in us; and all they have sown into our lives.

Pastor Rodney Howard Browne and Adonica have been a tremendous encouragement to Martha and I. They have received us with open arms and have given Godly advice and counsel to us. More importantly they have brought back to our live the FIRE of God and the zeal for souls. They have stirred up the flame and challenged us to allow the Holy Spirit to have free reign and control in our lives.

All of these individuals have given inspiration and counsel, but most of all, are friends have encouraged me in my spiritual walk and growth in God. The one thing these people demonstrated was the attitude to serve--to serve God and to serve God's people. There is no real service to God apart from serving His people.

In *Ephesians 4:11-16*, we see a marvelous depiction of the purpose of what has been called the five-fold ministry: the apostle, the prophet, the evangelist, the pastor, and the teacher. They are given as gifts to the Church, and gifts are given to be used. In this case, the gifts are used to serve the Church so it will mature and grow into the fullness of what God called it to be.

BIBLIOGRAPHY

Gundry, Robert H; A Survey of the New Testament: (Grand Rapids, MI.; Zondervan Publishing House, 1982).

W.E. Vine, An Expository Dictionary of New Testament Words, (Old Tappan, Fleming H. Revell, 1940), Vol. III.

James Strong: Strong's Exhaustive Concordance, Compact Edition; (Nashville, Abingdon, 1890); Hebrew and Chaldee Dictionary.

Michael Landsman; Supportive Ministries, (Bridge-Logos Publishers, Newberry, FL, 1987)

PRODUCTS AVAILABLE:

Saved to Serve   : $10.00

DVD Series (5 Disks) on Supportive Ministries: $50.00

CD Series (10 CD's) on Servant Leadership: $100.00

Dr. Landsman is available for Ministry and Church Consulting. To contact Dr. Michael Landsman: write or Email:

3490 North Key Drive #511C

North Fort Myers, Florida 33903 USA

drmichaelmc@gmail.com
michael.landsman65@gmail.com

Feel free to include your prayer requests and comments when you write.

WORLD OUTREACH BIBLE SCHOOLS
(W. O. B. S.)

A concept whose time has come!

W. O. B. S. has been designed for the local church that desires to establish a training center or Bible school for the equipping of their members. W. O. B. S. provides the local church and the students with quality faith based material that combines the truths of God's Word with practical applications to everyday life.

The students are not only a part of your local church school, but they are also connected with students worldwide. This curriculum also is being used in various locations around the world with schools in Europe, Africa, Scandinavia, the Caribbean, South America, and Asia.

In addition, the material is available for those who want to do the course on an individual basis as a distance learning course.

If you would like to know more about this, please contact Dr. Michael Landsman via email at

drmichaelmc@gmail.com

Made in the USA
Charleston, SC
23 February 2016